Teaching
Tall Tales

By Tracey West

SCHOLASTIC
PROFESSIONAL BOOKS

New York • Toronto • London • Auckland • Sydney

The author wishes to thank Katherine Noll

and Cathleen Bowley,

two tireless and talented researchers,

for all their help.

The tall tale stories and activity pages in this book may be reproduced for classroom use. No other part of this publication can be reproduced in whole or in part, or stored in a retrieval system or transmitted in any form or by any means, electronic, mechanical, photocopying, recording, or otherwise, without written permission of the publisher. For information regarding permission, write to Scholastic Inc., 555 Broadway, New York, NY 10012.

Cover design and illustration by Paulette Bogan
Interior design by Joy Jackson Childs
Interior illustrations by Paulette Bogan and Delana Bettoli;
maps by Solutions by Design, Inc.
ISBN: 0-590-36511-8
Copyright © 1998 by Tracey West
All rights reserved.
Printed in the U.S.A.

Contents

About This Book 4

Old Stormalong 8
Ocean Adventure (Writing) 10
Can You Fathom It? (Math) 10
Around the World (Geography) 11
A Whale of an Art (Art, History)............. 11
Map the Coast with Old Stormalong (Map) ..12

Johnny Appleseed 14
True Stories (Writing) 16
America's First Residents (History)............. 16
Dried Apple Snacks
    (Science, Social Studies, Math) 17

John Henry 18
Into the Future (Writing) 20
The Great Machine Race (Math) 20
Make a Railroad Time Line
    (History, Math) 21

Sal Fink 24
In the News (Writing)............................ 26
Where Does It Come From? (Geography) .. 27

Annie Christmas 28
Compare and Contrast (Writing) 30
Make a Mardi Gras Mask
    (Social Studies, Art) 30
Great American Rivers (Map) 32

Davy Crockett 34
Bragging and Boasting (Writing)................ 37
Speak Out! (Social Studies, Language Arts) 37

Pecos Bill and Slue-Foot Sue............ 38
Tell a Witty Whopper (Writing) 40
Find the Little Dipper (Science).................. 41

Paul Bunyan 42
Natural Wonders (Writing) 44
Map Your State (Geography) 45
Travel Paul Bunyan Country (Map) 46

Kana, the Hawaiian Giant 48
Stretching the Truth (Writing).................... 50
Breakfast for a Giant (Math)...................... 51
Make a Travel Guide (Geography)............... 51

Sedna of the Sea 52
Make a Myth (Writing) 54
Alaskan Animal Mobile
    (Science, Social Studies, Art) 54

Tall Tales Across the U.S.A
Poster and Game 56

Wrapping up the Theme 63

Resources .... Inside back cover

About This Book

John Henry swinging his mighty hammer. Johnny Appleseed whistling as he walks down a dirt road with a sack of seeds slung over his shoulder. Cowgirl Slue-Foot Sue riding a giant catfish. For many of us, these colorful images of larger-than-life characters have stayed with us since their tales were first told to us in childhood.

Tall tales may hold a special place in our hearts, but they also hold a special place in the classroom. Teaching tall tales has been a curriculum requirement in elementary classrooms for many years. Thanks to the tireless work of talented researchers, new tales and characters have been uncovered in recent years, giving teachers the opportunity to put a fresh spin on an old theme.

This book was written to help you breathe new life into your tall tale lessons. Inside, you'll meet some characters you may have never met before. You'll also find fun suggestions for teaching tall tales in a variety of curriculum areas, including language arts, history, geography, math, science, and art. The book contains all you'll need to teach a tall tale theme, but it's also ideal for combining with your favorite resources.

Inside the Book

This book contains 10 lessons about different tall tale characters. Each lesson contains tales and activities that can be done as a class, at a learning center, or at home. Here's what you'll find in each lesson:

- **The Tale** This is a 2-page reproducible tale about each character. Copies of each tale can be given to students before the lesson or combined into individual tall tale storybooks.

- **History Notes** Tall tales offer a unique perspective on our country's history. Each tale is followed by information that explains the tale's role in American history.

- **Language Arts Activities** These include a vocabulary review, comprehension and discussion questions, and a writing mini-lesson.

- **Additional Teaching Activities** Each tale is accompanied by activities related to other curriculum areas such as history, geography, math, science, and art.

- **Reproducible Maps** Some activities are accompanied by a reproducible map and activity page. Photocopy these and distribute to the class, place in a learning center, or assign as homework.

- **Resources** Related books are listed at the end of each tall tale lesson. For general resources about teaching tall tales and information on other tall tale characters, check the inside back cover of this book.

- **Tall Tales Poster** Besides serving as a focal point in your classroom or tall tale learning center, the poster can also be used as an interactive geography game. Turn to page 56 for game cards and rules. The poster is bound in the back of this book.

Using This Book

The integrated curriculum activities in this book make it possible to present the topic as a theme unit. To introduce the theme, use the lesson on page 6 with the whole class. The lessons about individual characters can be used with the whole class or after dividing the class into small groups.

The tales in this book begin on the east coast and end in the northwest. You may wish to follow this east-west progression, or you may prefer to use only those lessons that focus on your geographic area or that relate to particular areas of study. Before teaching each lesson, preview the activities and make a list of materials you'll need so that everyone can participate.

Use the reproducible tales to make a tall tales storybook for each student. Make one copy of each tale for each student in your class. Arrange the tales in the order in which you plan to teach them. Have students make and decorate front and back covers using pieces of tagboard. Then show them how to put all the pages together, punch the left side with a three-hole punch, and tie a piece of yarn in each hole. Students can use their finished storybooks throughout the theme.

What Is a Tall Tale?

Before introducing the topic of tall tales to students, it helps to look at the subject from a language arts point of view. How does a tall tale differ from a legend, a myth, or other types of stories? Use this overview to help answer students' questions.

● **Tall Tale** The one element common to all tall tales is exaggeration. Tall tales are always about the biggest, the fastest, and the strongest—they're larger than life. Most tall tales start out with a grain of truth that is blown way out of proportion by the storyteller, usually in a humorous way. The subjects of tall tales are often great individuals, but they're also about incredible animals or unbelievable storms. In the United States, tall tales have been told about real figures in history; they've started out as ordinary men and women; and they've even been invented by newspaper writers. A tall tale doesn't have to be historical; a fourth-grader recounting her summer vacation may in fact be telling a tall tale. Other names for tall tales include "windies," "whoppers," and "lies."

● **Folktale** A folktale is a story told in a particular place or region that has been passed down by word of mouth for generations. The exact time period and setting of a folktale is often murky. A tall tale can be a folktale, but not all folktales are tall tales.

A Note About the Tales in this Book

A variety of resources were used to adapt the tales for this book. Because of the word-of-mouth nature of tall tales, story details vary from source to source. Decisions had to be made about which details to include every step of the way. For example, how far did John Henry drill in his famous race against the steam drill? Was Old Stormalong a sea captain or just a sailor? In the end, details were chosen that seemed most common to all versions of the tale, made the story more interesting, and that were most appropriate for the elementary audience.

● **Folklore** The songs, traditions, customs, tales, riddles, sayings, and superstitions preserved orally by a group of people are known as folklore.

● **Legend** A legend is a story that reaches far back into history; it's usually believed to be historically true, but there's little or no historical fact to back it up. Robin Hood and King Arthur are examples of legends.

● **Myths** A myth is a type of story created by people to help explain the world around them, especially beliefs, practices, and natural phenomena. Why is the sky blue? Why is the turtle slow? These are the questions that myths answer. In this book, you'll find the Alaskan myth of Sedna of the Sea. Use this story to discuss the difference between myths and tall tales, as well as to explore the variety of stories that stem from our country's past.

The history of the United States is rich in all of these types of stories—tall tales, legends, and myths. In one way or another, students will have a chance to compare and think about all three types in this book. Primarily, though, they'll be having fun exploring the humor and exaggeration in some of the country's most famous tall tales.

Introducing Tall Tales

Here are some ideas for introducing tall tales to your class. Use one, or combine them to make a complete lesson:

● Begin by asking: *Do you know what a tall tale is?* If there is no response, ask students to guess what it might be. Is there a clue in the name that suggests what the tale might be like? Explain that tall tales are stories that use exaggeration—the characters and their actions might be based on truth, but they are enlarged to make an incredible story. Ask: *Can you think of any times that you or someone you know has exaggerated the truth? Why do you think people exaggerate?* Explain that one reason people exaggerate is to make a story more interesting, funny, or enjoyable.

● Lead the class in a fun exaggeration exercise. On the chalkboard, write: "My uncle is so big, _____." Lead off the exercise by filling in the sentence with some of your own ideas. (He uses a swimming pool for a cereal bowl; I can sleep in one of his shoes; etc.) Go around the room and encourage students to fill in the sentence with their own exaggerations. Try this with a variety of sentence starters. For example, "My walk to school is so long, _____." "I am such a good baseball player that _____."

● Use the Tall Tale Characters list (see page 7) to introduce the tall tale characters in this book to students. Discuss the characters with students to determine if they have any prior knowledge of them. You can also have students make predictions about what they think the characters will be like, based on their names and short descriptions.

Tall Tale Characters

Old Stormalong

This larger-than-life sailor fought sea monsters off the New England coast.

Johnny Appleseed

A gentle soul who traveled the midwest, he spread apple seeds wherever he went.

John Henry

The steel-driving railroad man became a legend after a race against a steam drill.

Sal Fink

This tough young woman proved trouble for an angry bear and a gang of river pirates.

Annie Christmas

Born in New Orleans, she became queen of the Mississippi River.

Davy Crockett

He was the frontier hero who went down in history as an expert woodsman.

Pecos Bill and Slue-Foot Sue

This bronco-riding couple was the wildest pair in the Wild West.

Paul Bunyan

He was the biggest lumberjack ever to reach the Northwest.

Kana
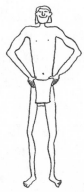
This Hawaiian giant could stretch his body out for miles.

Sedna

The courageous hero of this Eskimo myth is the mother of all sea creatures.

Old Stormalong

Long ago, just before George Washington became our first president and fireworks first lit up the sky on the Fourth of July, a boy named Alfred Bulltop Stormalong was born in what later became the state of Maine.

In those days, there were three things a boy could grow up to do. He could farm if he found a patch of land that wasn't too rocky. He could trap lobsters in the bays off of the Maine coast. Or he could sign on with a sailing ship and travel all over the world.

Now Alfred came from a farming family, but he longed to sail the sea. He stood for hours on tall rocks, searching for ships sailing from far away, until one day he realized that if he grew tall enough he'd be able to see even farther. So he made himself grow! By the time he was ten he stood six feet tall. Sailors, who used fathoms to measure the depths of the sea, said he stood at one fathom.

A few years later, Alfred signed on as a cabin boy with a whaling ship. On the ship's log he was listed as A.B. Stormalong, and to this day all sailors have the initials A.B.S. after their names, which stands for Able-Bodied Sailor.

After some time on the whaling ship, Stormalong realized that if he grew even taller he could spot whales far away. So he grew some more. Sure enough, soon after, he sighted a whole school of whales. The captain set sail, but the ship didn't get very far. She was stuck in the middle of the ocean. She wouldn't budge.

No one seemed to understand why the ship wouldn't move, but Stormalong had an idea. He tossed off his shirt and dove into the water. Suddenly, the water began to bubble and stir. The ship's crew watched in amazement as Stormalong emerged from the water in the clutches of a giant octopus.

Before the sailors knew what had happened, Stormalong was back on board and the octopus was sinking into the sea. When they asked him what had happened, Stormalong replied, "It was nothing. I swam underwater and I saw that the octopus had grabbed ahold of the ship with its eight long arms. So I tied a sailor's knot in each one. That monster won't be grabbing ships any time soon!"

When he got a little older, Stormalong signed on to another whaling ship. He was anxious to start harpooning whales, but he still had one problem—he was too big to fit into the small whaling boats. When a whale was sighted, the other sailors would jump into the small boats and row as close to the whale as they could so they could harpoon it from five fathoms away.

Stormalong wanted to harpoon a whale more than anything else, so he practiced and practiced until he could throw a harpoon 25 fathoms. He just leaned over the ship, threw his harpoon, and pulled the whale right in. His whale boat didn't go to waste, though. He used it as a bowl to hold his favorite supper—whale-and-shark chowder.

Stormalong loved life on the whaling ship, but he soon grew too big for the vessel and had to return to his family's farm in Maine. He was sad, and missed the ocean, until one day he heard word that a ship was being built—the *Albatross*.

The *Albatross* was the biggest ship the world had ever seen. It was so big that sailors used horses to travel around the decks. The ship's sails had to be sewn in the Sahara Desert so there would be room to spread them out.

Stormalong signed on as captain. By now he stood four fathoms high. On the *Albatross*, Stormalong was able to live out his lifelong dream. He sailed to mysterious and wonderful places all over the globe until his last days.

The End

Teaching Activities

About This Tale

While not based on a real person, the character of Alfred Bulltop Stormalong was inspired by the stories of the great American shipmen of the 18th century. His story first appeared in written form in 1933 in *Old Stormalong Yarns* by Charles Edward Brown.

History Notes

Old Stormalong's story is closely tied with the history of whaling. While whaling had been practiced in other parts of the world for about four thousand years, the United States saw a whaling boom off its northeastern shores in the 1750s. If Old Stormy were alive today, however, he'd be less eager to spear a whale with his harpoon. Over-hunting has decreased the whale population, and today many species of this great sea mammal are endangered.

Stormalong's tales also coincide with the American Revolution. In fact, one tale has him battling the British navy.

Vocabulary

bay: a small part of the ocean that is partly enclosed by land

cabin boy: a boy whose job it is to serve the other sailors on a ship

chowder: a thick stew made of seafood and vegetables

fathom: a unit of measurement that equals 6 feet, used by sailors to measure the depth of water

harpoon: a long spear, used in hunting large fish and whales

Questions

1. At what time in history does this story take place? (around the time of the American Revolution) What clues in the story tell you this? (reference to George Washington becoming president, and to the Fourth of July)

2. How did Stormalong become a giant? (He made himself grow so he could see things far away.)

3. How did Stormalong defeat the octopus? (He tied its arms with sailor's knots.)

4. Why was the *Albatross* the perfect ship for Stormalong? (It was the only ship in the world big enough to hold him.)

Writing Ocean Adventure

Have students rewrite part of Stormalong's story. Can they figure out another way Stormalong could have subdued the giant octopus or solved his whale-hunting problem?

Math Can You Fathom It?

The story explains that sailors use a unit of measurement called a fathom, which equals 6 feet. Have students convert the fathoms in the story into feet:

- Full grown, Stormalong stood 4 fathoms high. (24 feet)
- A normal sailor could throw a harpoon 5 fathoms. (30 feet)
- Stormalong could throw a harpoon 25 fathoms. (150 feet)

Ask: *How can you convert fathoms to feet?* (Multiply 6 feet by the number of fathoms.) Extend the activity by helping students experience the size of these fathom distances. Take the class out to the schoolyard and use a yardstick to measure, cut, and lay pieces of

string in a straight line, equal to the lengths given above.

Geography Around the World

Throughout his sailing career, Old Stormalong carried cargoes to India, China, Australia, Russia, Italy, and Australia. Show students a globe or world map. Beginning off the coast of Maine, have students plot a course around the world that Stormalong could have taken, with stops at each country along the way. Remind students that Stormy traveled by ship, and review the difference between land and water on the globe or map. Challenge students to figure out the shortest possible route Stormy could have taken by using a scale of miles to measure the route. Students can write out Stormalong's itinerary, or draw Stormy's path on a blank world map form.

Art • History A Whale of an Art

If Old Stormalong was anything like the other sailors of his time, he might have practiced the art of scrimshaw by scratching pictures into whalebone (trimmed baleen) and teeth. Whales may be endangered today, but a bar of soap makes a great scrimshaw substitute.

Materials
- bar of soap (1 per student)
- pencils
- watercolor or tempera paints
- paintbrushes
- paper towels

1. Have each student scratch a picture into the soap with a pencil and brush off the soap flakes.

2. Next, have students brush wet paint into the scratches, making sure the scratches are filled with paint.

3. Tell students to use a paper towel to rub off the extra paint. The paint will stay inside the scratches.

Reproducible Activity

Map the Coast with Old Stormalong
(pages 12–13)

This interactive map activity helps students build geography vocabulary as they explore the New England coast.

Answers: 1. 2; **2.** 6; **3.** 8; **4.** 3; **5.** 7; **6.** 9; **7.** 1; **8.** 4; **9.** 10; **10.** 5

Resources

Book of the American Revolution by Howard Egger-Bovet and Marlene Smith Baranzini (Little, Brown, 1994) This Brown Paper Schoolbook provides a rich overview of the historical period that gave rise to Old Stormalong.

Whaling Days by Carol Carrick (Clarion, 1993) A history of whaling from its importance as an industry in colonial America to its role as the focus of present-day conservation efforts.

Name _____

Map the Coast with Old Stormalong

An able-bodied sailor like Old Stormalong would know every inch of water near his home coast. A coast is where the edge of land meets a body of water. The map on page 13 shows the coast of New England, where Stormy lived and sailed. Read the list of water words below. Then use the clues to match the water words to where they belong on the map.

Water Words

bay: a small part of the ocean that is partly enclosed by land

cape: a point of land that juts into a body of water; sometimes also called a peninsula

cove: a small bay

harbor: a part of a body of water that is protected by land and deep enough for ships to safely anchor there

island: land completely surrounded by water on all sides

lake: a large body of water with land all around it

mouth: the place where a river empties into another body of water

ocean: a large body of salt water that covers a big part of the earth's surface

river: a large stream of water that flows into another body of water

tributary: a small river or stream that connects to a larger river or stream

Clues

In the blank boxes, write the number of the place on the map that best matches each description. Then fill in the name next to its number on the map.

1. ☐ The New England coast touches the Atlantic **Ocean.**

2. ☐ Swans **Island** lies northeast of Portland, Maine.

3. ☐ You'll find Boston Inner **Harbor** tucked safely inside the city.

4. ☐ The Penobscot **River** flows into the Atlantic Ocean.

5. ☐ If you sailed east from Boston, you'd reach Massachusetts **Bay.**

6. ☐ **Cape** Cod looks like a boot in southeastern Massachusetts.

7. ☐ You'll find Graham **Lake** southeast of Bangor, Maine.

8. ☐ The Piscataquis is a **tributary** of the Penobscot River.

9. ☐ Pigeon **Cove** lies northeast of Boston and south of Portland, Maine.

10. ☐ The **mouth** of the Penobscot River is south of Bangor, Maine.

Teaching Tall Tales   Scholastic Professional Books

The New England Coast

(Use with page 12.)

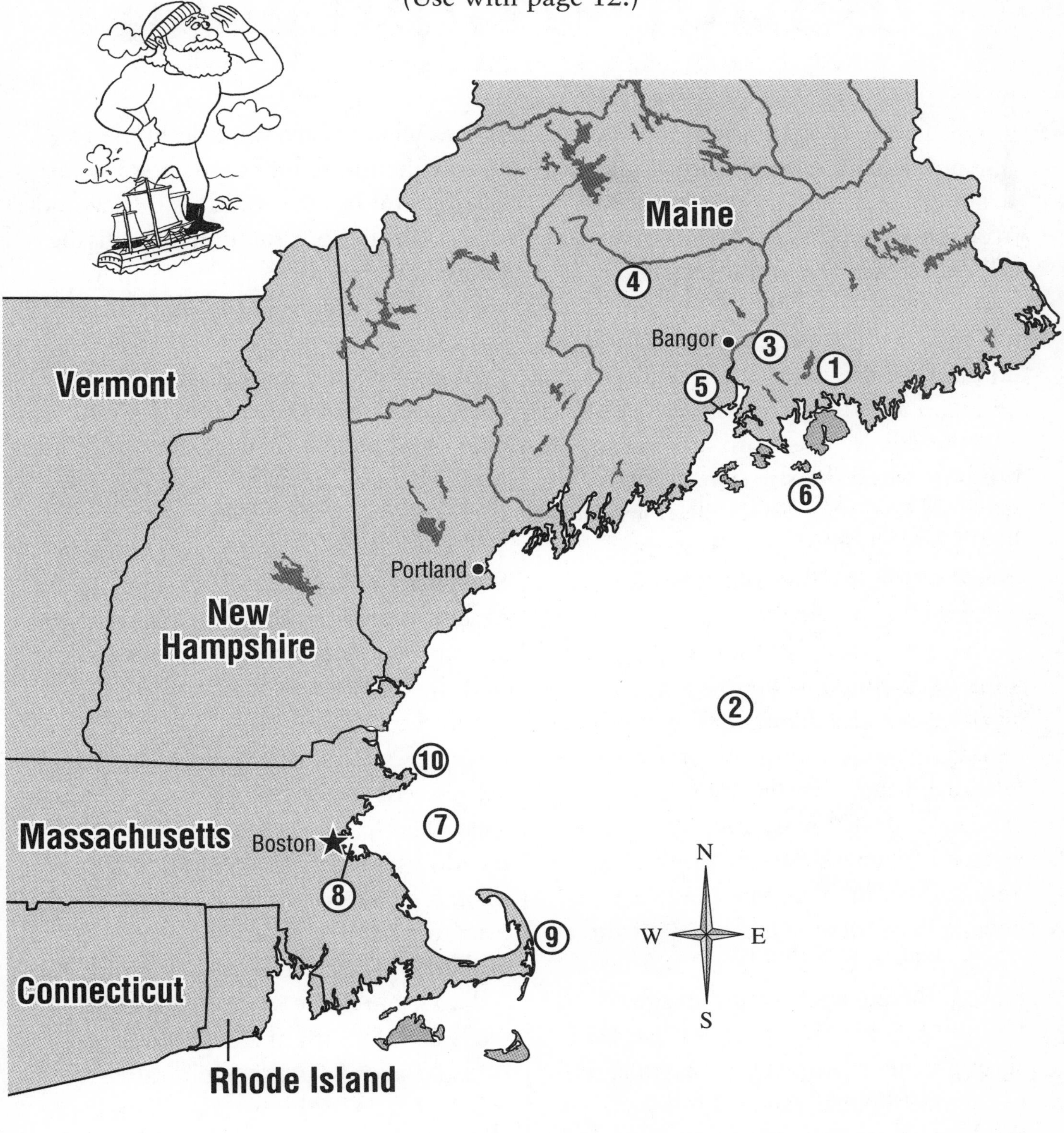

Maine

Vermont

Bangor ● ③ ①

⑤

④

New
Hampshire

Portland ●

⑥

②

⑩

Massachusetts Boston ★

⑦

⑧

⑨

Connecticut

N

W ✦ E

S

Rhode Island

Johnny Appleseed

If you were to take a look at Johnny Appleseed, you might not think this skinny man was a great hero. But over the years, his legend has grown as tall as the apple trees he grew.

Of course, when Johnny was born at the end of the American Revolution, he didn't have the name Appleseed yet. His parents named him Jonathan Chapman, and the day he was born a beautiful rainbow filled the sky. The colors of the rainbow lit up the apple blossoms in the family orchard, and from that moment Johnny loved apples more than anything in the world.

That's not exactly true—Johnny loved animals as much as he loved apples. As a young boy, he'd spend all day in the woods, making friends with the creatures who lived there. Birds, squirrels, raccoons, deer, foxes, and even snakes were all Johnny's friends. Johnny loved animals so much that he made a vow never to eat them—and he never did.

When he was 23, Johnny and his family moved west to Pittsburgh, Pennsylvania. Many pioneers passed through the city on their way to settle in the midwest. It made Johnny sad to think of all those families moving to

places where there were no apple trees. It was then that Johnny decided what his mission in life would be. He would travel throughout the midwest, giving away apple seeds, planting as many seeds as he could, and taking care of apple trees.

Johnny waited until the Pittsburgh cider presses had turned apples into cider, and picked through the sticky leftover mess to gather the seeds. He carefully dried them and put them in sacks. Then he set out on his mission. Some say he kept the sacks in a bag he carried on his back. Others said he had so many seeds he loaded up two canoes, tied the canoes together, and set off down the Ohio river.

Johnny's fame slowly grew. He gave away seeds for free to pioneers heading west. The rest he planted in fields, meadows—wherever he could. When the trees had grown he returned to the orchards to care for them. Johnny's orchards grew mainly in Ohio and Indiana, but some say he spread his seeds as far south as Tennessee and as far west as the Rocky Mountains.

Before long, Johnny gave himself the name "Appleseed." He didn't like to

take money for his work, so he was too poor to buy clothes. He wore a flour sack for a shirt and never wore shoes. Tales of his adventures traveled as far as he did. Most stories had to do with his kindness to animals.

Once, when Johnny was walking through the woods, he came upon a wolf with its leg caught in a trap. The wolf's eyes were filled with pain. Johnny slowly approached it. That wolf would have growled at any other human being, but not Johnny. Johnny gently released its leg from the trap and took care of it until it was well. From then on, the wolf followed Johnny around like a puppy dog.

On another cold night, Johnny was huddled around a campfire, trying to keep warm. Buzzing mosquitoes were attracted to the bright flames. Many flew into the fire and died. Johnny felt so bad for them that he doused out the fire with water. He shivered through the rest of the night.

Besides bringing apples to the midwest, Johnny brought something else— a message of peace. In Johnny's time, pioneers traveled through and settled on the land of Native Americans. The native people were angry with the pioneers for taking the land they had lived on for so many years. Many battles were fought and people killed during this time.

Johnny didn't like to see people hurt any more than he did mosquitoes. He became friends with many Native Americans in his travels, and he did what he could to prevent fighting on both sides.

Johnny made the whole country his home until the end of his life at the age of 71. When he died, he was found resting peacefully under an apple tree. Some say his ghost still wanders through apple orchards, looking after his precious apples forever.

The End

Teaching Activities

About This Tale

Johnny Appleseed is one of many tall tale characters who is based on a real person. Jonathan Chapman lived from 1774–1845 and did travel the midwest with his sacks of apple seeds. Arguments still exist about whether he is a true American hero, or a well-meaning eccentric.

History Notes

Born at the tail end of the American Revolution, Johnny Appleseed's life spans an exciting period in American History—the start of the settlement of the west. In 1803, during the time of Johnny Appleseed's travels, the United States purchased the Louisiana Territory from France, increasing the size of the country by 140 percent.

Vocabulary

cider: juice produced by squeezing apples through a press

mission: a plan or activity

orchard: an area where fruit trees are planted

pioneers: the first people from the east to travel west in North America

vow: a promise

Questions

1. What was Johnny's mission? (to plant apple trees all over the country)

2. Johnny Appleseed wasn't a powerful giant. Why do you think his story is a tall tale? (He was an ordinary person who did extraordinary things.)

3. What parts of Johnny's life do you think might have been exaggerated? (The rainbow at his birth, having a wild animal as a pet, and saving the lives of mosquitoes are all things that could have been exaggerated, as well as how far and wide Johnny traveled.)

4. What parts of the story support the statement that Johnny Appleseed was kind to animals? (He didn't eat them; he saved a hurt wolf; he put out a fire to save mosquitoes.)

Writing True Stories

Use Johnny Appleseed's story to introduce biography. Ask students to choose a real-life person whom they admire—a family member, a friend, or a favorite actor or sports star. Have students write a simple one-page biography that gives the basic facts about that person's life: where and when the person was born, family information, and details about what that person has done to inspire them. Then have students try rewriting the biography and adding exaggerated details. When they're done, they'll have turned their subject into a tall tale character.

History America's First Residents

As is evident in the story of Johnny Appleseed, no discussion of westward expansion is complete without considering the impact of settlement on Native American life. Have students use the local library or historical society to find out which Native American group(s) first lived in your state or region. Divide the class into small groups and have each group research and report on one aspect of that tribe's life: food, shelter, clothing, art and music, traditions, and tribal history.

With older students, explore the question of the effect the settlers had on Native Americans. Hold a class debate on the topic or challenge students to suggest ways in which expansion could have been handled differently.

Dried Apple Snacks

A traveler like Johnny Appleseed knew the importance of packing food that lasts a long time and is easy to eat and carry. Johnny himself would have approved of these packable apple snacks:

Materials
- apples (1 per student)
- knife
- string
- cheesecloth

1. Peel and core the apples, then slice each apple horizontally into 1/4-inch rings. (adult only)

2. Thread the apple rings through a long piece of string. (It's better to use one long piece of string for the whole class, rather than for each student.) Tie the string between two chairs in a warm, dry area. Near a radiator is a good spot. Pull the string until it is taut. The apple rings shouldn't touch one another. Cover the apple rings with cheesecloth to protect them from dust and bugs.

3. Ask students to predict: *What will happen to the apple rings in about two weeks? What do you think they will look like?* If possible, weigh the apple rings before stringing them. Ask: *Do you think the weight of the rings will change? Why?*

4. In about two weeks, check the rings. They will look dry and wrinkled and have a chewy texture. Ask students: *How did the apple rings change?* (They dried when the water in them evaporated.) *Where did the water go?* (It turned into water vapor.) *Why didn't the apple rings rot or turn moldy?* (Water encourages mold growth; drying prevents the mold from forming.)

5. If you weighed the apple rings before stringing them, weigh them again now. The rings should weigh less than before. Ask: *What do you think caused the change in weight?* (the loss of water)

6. To keep the apple rings fresh for snacking, remove from the string and store in a sealed container or plastic bag.

Resources

Johnny Appleseed by Steven Kellogg (Morrow Books, 1988) A traditional look at the gentle hero, suitable for younger readers.

The Real Johnny Appleseed by Camille Hodges (Albert Whitman, 1995) Wood engravings enhance this rich examination of Jonathan Chapman's life, which spanned the period from the American Revolution to the westward expansion.

John Henry

The night John Henry was born, just before the Civil War, a great black cloud covered the moon. Winds blew, the sky thundered, and a streak of forked lightning lit up the sky. Instead of hiding from the storm, all of the animals in the woods gathered around the Henrys' cabin.

Years later, after John Henry became a legend, people would say that he was born with a hammer in his hand. No one knows for sure, but what they do know is that John Henry was a big, strong baby.

As soon as he could walk, John Henry grabbed his father's heavy hammer and gave it a good swing. He used that hammer on nails and wood, and on steel to break rocks.

"When I grow up," John Henry would say, "I'm going to make a living with a hammer in my hand."

When the Civil War was over, John Henry married his girlfriend, Polly Ann, and set out to follow his dream. It wasn't long before he found it. Back in those days, railroad companies were clearing the way for railroad tracks all over the country. The only trouble was, plenty of mountains and large rocks got in their way. They needed strong workers to hammer steel spikes into the thick rocks and make deep holes. When a hole was big enough, they'd stuff it with dynamite and blast open an even bigger hole.

John Henry came upon a crew working for the Chesapeake and Ohio Railroad. When he saw the men lifting giant hammers that gleamed in the sun, he knew what he was born to do. John Henry approached the crew's boss, Captain Tommy, and asked for a job. When Captain Tommy saw what John Henry could do with a hammer he hired him on the spot.

Working with a twenty-pound hammer, John Henry was the fastest steel driver on the crew. No one could do better. But one day, a man with a steam-operated drill came to Captain Tommy. He said his machine could drill faster than three men. On top of that, it didn't need to eat or sleep.

Captain Tommy and the crew just laughed. They knew that John Henry was faster than at least four men. So Captain Tommy made a deal with the steam-drill operator: He'd bet that John Henry could drill farther than the machine in nine hours. If John Henry

lost, Captain Tommy would buy the drill. If John Henry won, he'd get the steam drill for free, plus five hundred dollars.

The steam-drill operator agreed. He didn't think any man alive could beat his machine. Captain Tommy asked John Henry if he would take the challenge, and John Henry didn't hesitate. He didn't want to lose the job he loved to a machine.

The next morning, the race began. The steam drill worked on the left side of the rock. Its giant boiler sat alongside, chugging out the steam to make the drill work. John Henry worked on the right side of the rock, pounding on the steel with a hammer in each hand.

One hour, two hours passed—and John Henry kept pounding away. Three hours, four hours—and John Henry kept going. A large crowd gathered to watch the race. Polly Ann brought him water to drink from a dipper.

Five hours, six hours passed. The steam drill chugged away. Everyone thought John Henry would slow down, but he didn't. Seven hours, eight hours, and John Henry was still pounding away.

By the ninth hour, the steam drill began to cough and sputter. John Henry was drenched in sweat. His large arms were weary. But he never gave up.

Finally, the race was over. The steam drill stopped chugging, and John Henry stopped swinging. A judge came to measure how far each had drilled. The steam drill had drilled nineteen-and-a-half feet. But John Henry had drilled 20 feet into the rock. He had won.

John Henry stumbled out of the tunnel in the rock as the sun was setting. The crowd clapped and cheered—and then let out a cry. John Henry had collapsed on the ground. His strong heart had stopped. He still held a hammer in each hand. The morning he was buried a great black cloud covered the sun, just like the cloud that covered the moon the day he was born.

To this day, people remember John Henry's story, not because of his death, but because of his amazing life.

The End

Teaching Activities

About This Tale

Between 1870 and 1873, workers on the Chesapeake and Ohio Railroad tunneled through the Allegheny Mountains in West Virginia, using a steam drill for the first time. There may have been an ex-slave named John Henry working on the crew, but there is no proof that the steam drill contest ever took place. His story began in the form of folk songs and ballads.

History Notes

In 1872, when John Henry's story takes place, more than 5,000 African Americans lived and worked in West Virginia. At the same time, the railroad industry was booming, having replaced steamboats and turnpikes as the fastest and most efficient way to transport goods around the country. The difficult, dangerous work of laying the tracks was performed by thousands of Chinese, Italian, and German immigrants, as well as recently freed sleeves like John Henry.

Vocabulary

hesitate: to hold back

sputter: to squirt liquid; to make popping sounds

steam drill: an instrument powered by steam, and used for making holes in hard objects

Questions

1. Why do you think John Henry accepted the challenge against the steam drill? (Answers may include: He didn't want to lose his job.)

2. Why might railroad workers have invented a hero like John Henry? (Answers may include: workers wanted a hero to admire; they feared being replaced by machines.)

3. Compare the account of John Henry's birth with that of Johnny Appleseed's (see page 14). How are they similar? (Both were marked by natural phenomena.) Strange or wonderful happenings at the birth of a character are common occurences in tall tales. Why do you think this might be? (It's a signal to readers that there's something extra-special about the character; it sets the tone for the story.)

Writing Into the Future

The struggle of man against machine is a common literary theme. Lead students in a discussion about how machines have changed our lives. What do they think happens when machines replace humans on the job? Is that a good or bad thing? Use the discussion as an opportunity to explore the genre of science fiction. Ask students to imagine what might happen if machines started taking over all jobs and to write a story about it. They may wish to rewrite the John Henry tale, but set it in the future.

Math The Great Machine Race

John Henry's race against the machine was a 9-hour struggle and a test of will. You can hold a great machine race in your own classroom to give students a feel for John Henry's experience.

Materials
- 2 stopwatches or watches with second hands
- computer, typewriter, calculator, electric pencil sharpener, blender and/or other machines of your choice

1. As a class, brainstorm a list of events that students could do to test themselves against machines. For example:

- **Word Whiz:** One student writes out the words to the Pledge of Allegiance by hand while another types it into a computer or with a typewriter.
- **Sharp Attack:** One student sharpens a new pencil on a hand-held sharpener while another uses an electric or crank-operated pencil sharpener.
- **Number Crunch:** One student adds, subtracts, or multiplies a set of numbers by hand while another does the same thing on a calculator.
- **Art Smart:** One student draws a picture of a dog by hand, while another uses a computer's illustration program.
- **Shake Down:** One student makes a milk shake by mixing together milk and ice cream in a closed container, while another uses a blender.

2. After you've made your list, gather all the materials you'll need. You may wish to set up different events in different parts of the classroom.

3. Divide the class into two groups: humans (or John Henrys) and machine operators. Each team should appoint two official timekeepers, and decide who will perform what task in each event.

4. Make a score sheet to record event results:

The Great Machine Race

Event	Humans	Machines
Word Whiz	46 seconds	51 seconds
Sharp Attack	8 seconds	2 seconds
Number Crunch		
Art Smart		
Shake Down		

5. Let the games begin! If necessary, review using a stopwatch with timekeepers.

6. When all the results are in, discuss the outcomes. How many events did the machines win? How many events did the humans win? Extend the discussion by asking: *What does this tell you about why machines were invented? Are machines always better than humans? What things do you think humans will always be better at?*

7. Extend the math by having students plot the results on a bar or pie graph.

History • Math

Make a Railroad Time Line

Whether or not John Henry was a real-life hero or a made-up character, his legend is an important part of the history of America's railroads. Students can practice their research skills to make a time line showing John Henry's race and other great moments in railroad history.

1. Assign students the task of researching key moments in the history of American railroads.

Good sources of information include encyclopedias, nonfiction books, and the Internet. If you prefer, give students the list of questions on reproducible page 23 as a guide. (Encourage them to add other facts that they find interesting.)

Make a Railroad Time Line
(page 23)

Answers: 1. 1830, the Baltimore and Ohio Railroad; **2.** Peter Cooper, 1830; **3.** 1831, Charleston and Hamburg line; **4.** 1856, it was the longest railroad in the country so far, and it was built mainly by immigrants; **5.** 1856, it spanned the Mississippi River and connected the eastern and western United States for the first time; **6.** 1861, railroads transported troops and supplies to both sides; **7.** 1869; **8.** 1914, after World War I, as more people used cars to get around.

2. Once students have gathered their information, have them plot these great moments on a time line. Explain that a time line is a visual device that shows how events in history unfolded. A time line is usually divided into equal sections marked by vertical lines. Each vertical line represents a year. Larger lines are used to indicate years ending in zero and five.

3. Decide if you will combine students' research to make one large class time line, or if you will have students make time lines individually. For a class time line, you may wish to use a long roll of bulletin board paper that can be stretched around the classroom. For individual time lines, have students tape together sheets of paper, end to end.

4. Review the information students have collected. To start, make a list of just the dates. Use the list to decide how long your time line needs to be and how far apart your year markers should be. For example, you might label only numbers ending in zero (1830, 1840, 1850) but leave nine one-year markers in between each number with plenty of room to record events. Better yet, why not make your time line look like a railroad track, with planks for year markers?

5. Write a short description of each event above or below the correct year marker. If there is room, students can decorate the time line with images illustrating each great moment.

Resources

America's First Railroads by Tim McNeese (Crestwood House, Macmillan Publishing, 1993) This nonfiction chronicle of early railroads will help students put John Henry's story in a historical perspective.

John Henry by Julius Lester (Dial Books, 1994) This fully illustrated tale turns the hero's tragic end into a cause for wonder and celebration with a message of hope from John Henry.

First Steam Engine transports passengers 1831 Illinois Central RR built largest in U.S. 1856

1830 1840 1850 1860

Name_____

Make a Railroad Time Line

Research the answers to the questions below. Add other facts about key moments in the history of American railroads, too. Then use this information to make your railroad time line.

1. When did the first American railroad open for business?
_____
_____

2. Who invented the first railroad steam engine, and in what year?
_____
_____
_____

3. When did the first steam-powered engine begin transporting passengers?
_____
_____

4. When was the Illinois Central Railroad company completed, and why was it important?
_____
_____
_____
_____

5. When was the Rock Island Railroad company completed, and why was it important?_____
_____
_____
_____

6. When did the Civil war begin, and why might it belong on a railroad time line?_____
_____
_____
_____
_____

7. When did the final spike connect the Union Pacific and Central Pacific railroads?_____
_____

8. When did railroads begin to decline? Why?_____
_____
_____

Add other key moments in American railroad history below or on the back of this page.
_____
_____
_____

Sal Fink

Almost 200 years ago, long before you were born, and your mother was born, and even before her mother was born, flat boats called keelboats traveled up and down the Mississippi and Ohio Rivers. If you were to take a walk along one of those riverbanks, you'd see the strong boat men straining their muscles to row and pull the heavy boats upstream. And if you were lucky, you'd get a glimpse of one strong woman standing proudly on deck, her dark hair gleaming in the sun.

That woman was Sal Fink, and working on a keelboat came naturally to her. Her father was Mike Fink, the king of all the keelboat men and the roughest, toughest man ever to ride the rivers. People say that he was half-horse, half-alligator, because he was as strong as a horse and just as mean and scary as an alligator.

If the story about Mike was true, then that would make Sal one-quarter alligator herself. That would explain a lot. Even as a little girl, Sal was known for her amazing feats. Some say she fought a duel with a thunderbolt once, and the thunderbolt lost. And everyone along the river remembered seeing young Sal riding downstream on the water on the back of an alligator. She stood upright, keeping her balance, and sang "Yankee Doodle" all the way.

Sal was at home on the river, but she was also right at home in the woods. Like her mother, Peg, Sal was a great hunter. She loved to go into the woods to hunt for meat for the supper table and furs to make clothes and blankets for the cold winters. But the dark woods were usually where she'd get into the most trouble.

Once, while out hunting, young Sal heard a noise in a big hollow tree.

When she stuck her head in to investigate, she found herself face to face with an angry mother bear and two cubs. Sal tried to run away—she knew better than to bother a mother with her cubs—but she was too late. The bear attacked her with her sharp claws, and little Sal fought back with her bare hands. In the end, the bear was no match for Sal Fink.

Sal felt just awful. She hadn't wanted to hurt the bear, but she had to save her own skin. She took the two cubs home with her and raised them as her own. They followed her everywhere from that day on.

You'd think after wrestling with a bear Sal would stay clear of those woods, but that didn't stop her. Sal kept hunting in the woods until she was grown.

One day, Sal was hunting wildcats when a band of 50 river pirates jumped out from behind the trees and tied her up tight. It seems they had a score to settle with her pa, Mike Fink, and they planned on holding her for ransom.

Now Sal was as angry as she had ever been in her life, but she kept calm until the moment was right. The pirates took her back to their hideout in a cave. When night fell, they lit a fire. One by one, the pirates fell asleep. That's when Sal made her move.

Sal burst open the ropes that bound her as if they were apron strings. One by one, she tied each pirate's arms and legs together with the pieces of rope. Then she threw them all into the fire, just to make sure they woke up.

The pirates yelped and struggled to get free. Before Sal left, she grabbed the gold that the pirates had stolen from the keelboats. Then she ran out of that cave and headed home, back to her bear cubs, and back to ride the rivers with her famous father.

The End

Teaching Activities

About This Tale

Not much is known about Sal Fink, except that her father was real-life riverboat man Mike Fink, who lived from 1770–1823. The exaggerated stories of the Fink family were popular in newspapers from 1820 until about the 1840s.

History Notes

In the early nineteenth century, riverboats were the chief method of transporting food, furs, and other goods around the country. Flatboats and keelboats were the first riverboats to carry large shipments of goods up and down the rivers. Going downstream was the easy part, and flatboats, which were about 40 to 80 feet long and 7 to 10 feet wide, only made the downstream trip. Once they reached their destinations, they were chopped apart and their wood was used for lumber.

Keelboat

Keelboats, on the other hand, made the trip back upstream. It wasn't easy, and a strong crew was needed to row, pole, and even tow the boats back up. To work a keelboat with her father, Sal Fink would have had to have been as strong and tough as the stories say she was.

Vocabulary

duel: a fight between two people

keelboat: a flat-bottomed riverboat that is rowed, towed, or pulled

pirate: a person who robs from others traveling in boats

ransom: an amount of money paid to free a person held captive

Questions

1. Why did Sal Fink ride a keelboat? (Because her father, Mike Fink, was "king of the keelboats.")

2. What happened to the mother bear in the story? What does the line "the bear was no match for Sal Fink" mean? (Sal killed the bear in the fight to save her own life.)

3. Did Sal feel good about killing the bear? Support your answer. (Sal felt awful; she took care of the baby cubs.)

4. What mistakes did the river pirates make? (They underestimated Sal's strength; they all fell asleep at once.)

5. What words could you use to describe a person who was "part alligator"? (answers will vary, but may include: mean, dangerous, frightening, tough, strong, sneaky, a good swimmer, etc.)

Writing — In the News

Extra! Extra! Sal Fink Ties up River Pirates! In the early nineteenth century, tales of Sal Fink's adventures entertained newspaper readers across the country. Invite students to travel back in time and turn one of Sal's adventures into a newspaper article.

1. Ask each student to choose an adventure from the story to write about.

2. Explain that most newspaper articles are written to present the facts about a story in order, from most important to least important. Students can begin by making a list of the important facts in the story that they want to present in their articles.

3. Newspaper articles try to answer "the 5 Ws and an H": Who the story is about; What happened; When it happened; Where it hap-

pened; Why it happened; and How it happened. Have students check to make sure all of these categories are answered by their facts.

4. The first paragraph of a newspaper story is called a *lead*. Encourage students to write a lead that not only tells the most important facts, but grabs a reader's attention.

5. In a real newspaper story, all facts must be backed up by a source—a person or document that proves that something really happened. Encourage students to add quotes to their stories from "eyewitnesses." What might a pirate say about his encounter with Sal? Would a chipmunk watching Sal fight the mother bear have something to say about it? You may wish to have students pose as different characters to be interviewed by student reporters.

Geography **Where Does It Come From?**

As in Sal Fink's time, goods today are still transported on America's rivers, but planes, trucks, and trains are also used. The ingredients in the lunch your students ate today probably came from all over the country. Challenge students to see what they can find out about where the items in their lunch came from.

1. Have students make a list of everything in their lunch today, including food, paper bags, and utensils.

2. Tell students to put the items on a chart like the one shown here. Ask them to try to figure out where each item came from and how it got to them. They may find some answers in the library, by looking at packages, and even by writing to the company that processed, packaged, or made the items.

Where Does It Come From?		
Item	From	How
tuna	Pacific Ocean	boat, train
bread	Delaware	truck
celery	California	truck
mayonnaise	Illinois	truck
milk	Delaware	truck

3. Have students compare charts with their classmates. Ask: *What method of transportation is most common? How do you think your lunch might change if it included only items made or grown in your community?*

Resources

Biography of a River: The Living Mississippi by Edith McCall (Walker and Company, 1990) A look at the history of the river, from the travels of early explorers to modern-day preservation efforts.

Mike Fink: A Tall Tale by Steven Kellogg (Morrow Junior Books, 1992) This colorful picture book tells the story of Sal's famous father.

Annie Christmas

Now everyone knows that there are no kings or queens in the United States; but folks in New Orleans, Louisiana might tell you something different. They know that a long time ago lived a woman named Annie Christmas, and she was queen of the Mississippi River.

Annie stood six feet eight inches tall. Her towering height, combined with her beautiful dark skin, made Annie Christmas a woman you weren't likely to forget.

Annie spent all her time carrying food and supplies up and down the southern part of the Mississippi River on her keelboat, and she knew every drop of its brown muddy water. When her keelboat traveled downriver, she could pole it faster than any man, and when it traveled back upstream, she could pull it against the current with her strong arms.

Before her husband died, Annie found time to have 12 strong sons, each 7 feet tall. But taking care of her large family didn't keep Annie away from the river she loved.

Most men didn't like the fact that there was a woman on the river who was so much bigger and stronger than they were. But if any of them tried to pick a fight over it, they learned their lesson awfully fast. Annie's sons would have gladly stuck up for her, but she didn't need them to. She simply whupped any man who caused her trouble. Annie strung a bead on a necklace for every man she beat in a fight. Before she died, they say that necklace was 30 feet long.

Annie worked hard on the river every day, but once in a while she liked to have a little fun. So one night she put on her best red dress, stuck some colorful feathers in her hair, and rowed her keelboat out to a fancy paddleboat. She used a rope to attach her keelboat to the bigger boat.

Annie planned to spend the night laughing and having a good time on that paddleboat, but that wasn't to be. The captain of that paddleboat was not happy at all about having the toughest woman in New Orleans on his boat. He didn't like to be around anyone who was stronger or smarter than he was— especially a woman. He scowled and snarled at Annie all night long.

The weather seemed to match the captain's mood. An angry storm was brewing, and the paddleboat began to

rock on the swollen waters of the river.

Soon the paddleboat came to a new channel—a shortcut made in the land for boats to travel through. Annie warned the captain that the channel was too small, that the boat would never make it, but the stubborn captain wouldn't listen. He steered that paddleboat right into the channel as the water churned and kicked around them. The boat snagged on twisted tree roots and sandbars.

the darkness behind her. Annie poled the keelboat out of the dangerous channel as the passengers cheered. But the night was not over yet. The storm was still kicking up, and Annie needed to get everyone safely back to the port in New Orleans.

There was only one thing to do. Annie tied the keelboat rope around her waist, climbed on shore, and towed the boat back safely to New Orleans all by herself. The captain and his paddleboat

Annie Christmas couldn't take it anymore. She knew that the captain was leading them all to disaster. Fighting against the strong winds, she jumped up on her keelboat and invited anyone who wanted to to do the same. The passengers followed her, but the crew stayed behind with their captain. Annie untied the rope and poled the keelboat away from the paddleboat as fast as she could.

The paddleboat seemed to disappear in

were never seen again.

Annie's strength and courage that stormy night made her a legend up and down the river. After that night she lived a good long life, and when she finally died, everyone in New Orleans came to her funeral. Her sons put her coffin on a black boat and watched it float away on the Mississippi, the river that Annie Christmas called home.

The End

Teaching Activities

About This Tale

The story behind the creation of Annie Christmas reads like a tall tale itself. In the 1920s, two New Orleans newspaper writers were tired of hearing the tall tales floating around their city. They decided to write about a tall tale character so incredible that no one could possibly believe the story. Their plan backfired. The newspaper stories about Annie Christmas excited the imaginations of everyone in New Orleans, who made the strong, proud woman a true hero.

History Notes

The New Orleans that Annie Christmas inhabited was a thriving city. Founded in 1718 as a French Colony, the city was desirable because of its location on the banks of the Mississippi River, just 100 miles north of the Gulf of Mexico. It was (and still is) a port for ocean-traveling ships as well as American riverboats. By the late nineteenth century, the descendants of French, Spanish, and English colonists, American settlers, and former slaves lived side by side, sharing cultures and traditions.

Vocabulary

channel: a narrow steam of water with land on both sides, sometimes human-made

churned: stirred up violently

keelboat: a flat-bottomed riverboat that is rowed, towed, or pulled

paddleboat: a boat propelled by a large wheel

pole: to use a long stick or pole to move a boat forward; the pole is pushed into the river bottom, propelling the boat forward

sandbar: a ridge of sand built up by currents in a river

Questions

1. What makes Annie Christmas a tall tale character? (her incredible strength and the amazing feat of towing the keelboat by herself)

2. What did it mean that Annie's necklace was 30 feet long? (Each bead on the necklace stood for a man Annie had beaten in a fight, so a 30-foot necklace would mean that Annie had won many fights.)

3. Why wouldn't the paddleboat captain listen to Annie's warnings? (Answers may include: He didn't want to listen to a woman; he didn't like Annie because she beat up his friends.)

4. Was Annie loved by the people of New Orleans? How do you know? (Because everyone in the city came to her funeral when she died.)

Writing · Compare and Contrast

Annie Christmas and Sal Fink were both strong women who lived and worked on the Mississippi River (see Sal Fink, page 24). Ask students to write a paragraph comparing and contrasting the two heroes. In what ways were they different? In what ways were they alike? If Annie Christmas and Sal Fink had met, would they have become friends? Why or why not?

Social Studies · Art

Make a Mardi Gras Mask

Mardi Gras is a weeklong festival held every spring in Annie Christmas's hometown, New Orleans. People celebrate by dressing up in masks and costumes and marching in elaborate parades. Invite students to make their own Mardi Gras

masks. Tell them that animal masks are very popular. But they might also like to try making a mask of their favorite tall tale character.

Materials (for each student)

- 8 1/2-by-11-inch piece of thin cardboard (half of an old file folder works well)
- scissors
- markers, colored pencils, paint and paintbrushes
- decorating materials such as glitter, beads, sequins, craft feathers, fake fur, leaves
- 12-inch stick or ruler
- masking tape
- ribbon

1. Have students trace a mask shape onto cardboard.

2. Before cutting out the mask, encourage students to add ears, beaks, whiskers, or other features to the basic shape to make it look like their chosen character.

3. Tell students to cut out the mask pattern, hold the mask up to their face, mark eye holes, then cut them out.

4. Invite students to color the mask with markers, crayons, or paints. They can also glue on glitter, sequins, feathers, or other materials.

5. Have students tape the stick or ruler to the back of the mask to make a handle. For a colorful and festive effect, they can wind ribbon around the stick.

6. To wear the mask, have students hold it in front of their face.

Reproducible Activity

Great American Rivers
(pages 32–33)

This interactive map activity lets students identify major American rivers.

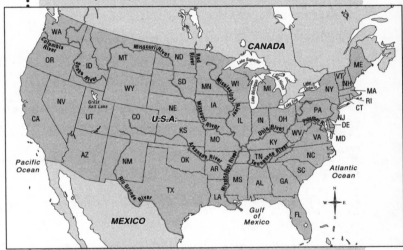

Answers:
1. The Ohio River;
2. The Rio Grande River;
3. The Potomac River;
4. 8 states: IA, NE, KS, MO, IL, SD, ND, MT;
5. The Mississippi River
6. The Arkansas River;
7. The Missouri and Mississippi Rivers;
8. The Columbia River

Resources

New Orleans: A Downtown America Book by Joan Kane Nichols (Dillon Press, 1989) A fun guide to New Orleans that takes readers on a tour of this colorful city.

The People Could Fly by Virginia Hamilton (Knopf, 1985) An illustrated collection of African-American folktales, many with tall tale elements.

Name_____

Great American Rivers

Use the clues below to label the rivers on the Great American Rivers Map (page 33). Then go to the "Figure It Out" section and answer the questions.

Clues

- The Mississippi River begins near the Great Lakes and flows south to the Gulf of Mexico.

- The Ohio River flows from Pennsylvania to Illinois.

- The Tennessee River flows through the state that shares its name.

- The Potomac River is the easternmost river shown on the map.

- The Arkansas River flows from Colorado to Arkansas.

- Part of the Snake River acts as a border between Oregon and Idaho.

- The Missouri River is the longest river in the United States.

- The Rio Grande River acts as a border between Texas and Mexico.

- The Red River acts as a border between North Dakota and Minnesota.

- The Columbia River is the westernmost river shown on the map.

Figure It Out

1. What river did pioneers travel on to get from the east to the midwest?

   _____

2. What river would you take to travel from Colorado to southern Texas? Trace the route on the map.

   _____

3. What river acts as a border between West Virginia, Maryland, and Virginia?

   _____

4. How many states does the Missouri River touch?_____

5. What river would you travel on if you wanted to transport goods from Wisconsin to Missouri?_____

6. What river on the map flows through Kansas and Oklahoma?

   _____

7. What rivers would you take to travel from northern Montana to Louisiana? Trace the route on the map._____

   _____

8. What river empties into the Pacific Ocean?

   _____

Teaching Tall Tales   Scholastic Professional Books

Name _____

The Great American Rivers Map
(Use with page 32.)

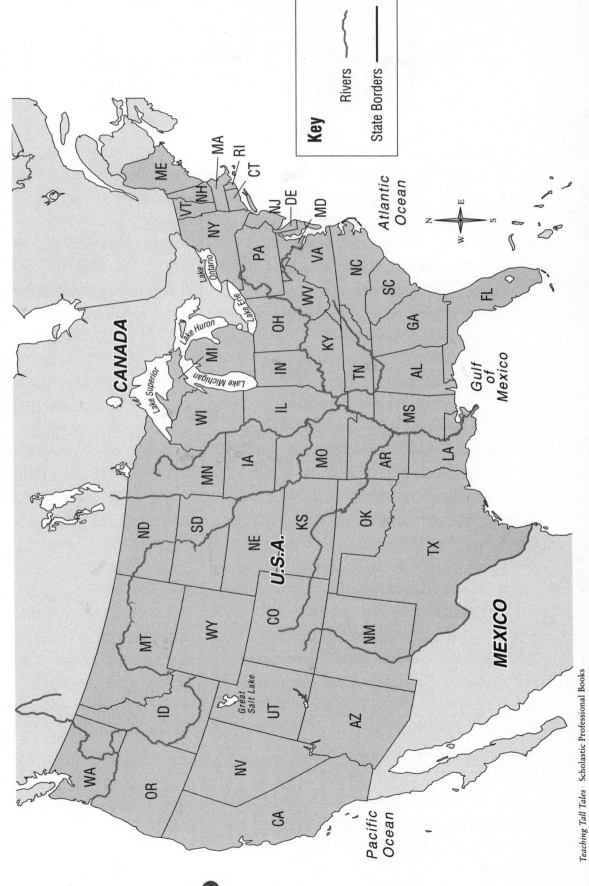

Davy Crockett

When Davy Crockett was born in 1786, not too many pioneers had ventured away from the country's eastern shores. But Davy's folks had, and so he was born on top of a mountain in Tennessee.

To live on the frontier in those days you had to be tough, and Davy was no exception. When he grew up, he would tell people that growing up in those woods had made him able to walk like an ox, run like a fox, swim like an eel, and wrassle any mountain lion that came his way. Davy claimed he could whip his weight in wildcats and wade across the Mississippi River.

How tough was Davy Crockett? Once, during a thunderstorm, people said he went outside and opened his mouth wide. He swallowed a thunderbolt in one gulp. For a month after that, he ate all of his food raw. The heat from the lightning cooked it right in his stomach.

Every animal in the woods knew how tough Davy was. Davy was a crack shot with his rifle, and always had food on the table for his family and warm animal skins on them for the cold frontier winters.

Davy's bragging made his name well-known in the Tennessee hills, so when it came time for the people of that state to send someone to Congress, they asked him to run for office. At first Davy didn't want to. He knew politicians had to give speeches, and he wasn't very good at this kind of thing. But he knew his people needed him, so he practiced making speeches on lonely hilltops until he was ready.

On election day, people gathered around outdoors as Davy gave his first speech. It was such a wonderful speech that everyone called out their votes for Davy at once. The animals of the woods were anxious for Davy to leave Tennessee and go to Washington, D.C., so they added their voices to the vote. And that's how Davy Crockett became a congressman.

Davy brought his pet alligator with him to Washington, D.C. and rode it wherever he went. His favorite thing about the nation's capital, besides meeting the

president, was a new invention called ice cream. He ate 20 quarts of it every day!

When Davy wasn't serving in Congress, he was busy saving the world. The first time he saved the world, a giant comet was hurtling toward Earth. Everyone hid in their cellars, waiting for the comet to hit. But not Davy. He climbed on top of the highest mountain he could find. When the comet sailed near him, he reached out and grabbed it with both arms. The comet moved and struggled, but Davy held fast. He turned that comet around and sent it back where it came from.

The second time Davy saved the world was the morning the sun never came up. The sky stayed pitch-black, and the air began to get colder and colder. Davy knew if he didn't do something fast the whole world would freeze over.

So Davy climbed up to the machinery that kept the sun moving around Earth.

There he found the sun, frozen between two large gears. Davy took off his raccoon-skin cap, scratched his head, and thought. Then he took a giant lump of bear grease from his bag and greased those gears until they shone. Slowly, the gears began to move, and the sun rose into the sky.

Saving the world twice was a pretty good trick, but that's not what made Davy Crockett a hero. In 1836, he joined the soldiers at the Alamo in Texas who were fighting for their independence from Mexico. Davy Crockett died fighting that day, but his legend will live on forever.

The End

Teaching Activities

About This Tale

Davy Crockett was a real person born on the frontier in 1786. He was a respected woodsman and soldier who served in Congress from 1827–32 and 1833–35, and became a legend after dying with the Texas revolutionaries at the Alamo in 1836. Davy could have gone down in history for these reasons alone, but he was a braggart who made up exaggerated tales about himself, turning his life into a series of great tall tales.

History Notes

When Davy Crockett was born, the American frontier was just taking shape. To survive on the frontier, settlers had to struggle to grow crops. For many, hunting was a crucial skill necessary for survival. Davy's sharpshooting skills made him a hero, but it's important to remember that his courage, humor, and political skills were also an important part of his character.

The settlement of the frontier was also the cause of conflict and bloodshed, not only between settlers and Native Americans but also with Mexico. When pioneers settled Texas in the early 1800s it was considered free territory by many countries, but Mexico had never recognized its independence. In 1846, Texas declared its independence and war broke out. Davy Crockett lost his life on March 6, 1836, defending the Alamo fort. Today many buildings and monuments in Texas bear his name.

Vocabulary

comet: a mass of ice and dust with a long tail that travels through space

Congress: the group of people elected to represent the people of the United States in government

gear: a wheel with teeth around the edges so that it can connect to other pieces in a machine

politician: a person who is part of a government

venture: to go on a difficult or dangerous journey

wrassle: slang for *wrestle*

Questions

1. Davy Crockett was a real person who told exaggerated stories about himself. Which details in this story do you think are true, and which do you think he invented? (It's true that he was born in Tennessee, became a congressman, and died fighting at the Alamo. All of the other details are either exaggerated or made up.)

2. Why did the animals in the woods want Davy to become a congressman? (If Davy was in Washington, D.C. he couldn't hunt them anymore.)

3. Davy thought it was important for politicians to be able to give good speeches. Do you agree? What examples of political speeches have you seen, heard of, or read about?

4. Use Davy's boasts in the story to review similes. Explain that a simile is a comparison using the word *like* or *as*. Challenge students to find examples of similes in the story. (Davy said he could walk like an ox, run like a fox, and swim like an eel.) What do these similes tell about him? (He was strong, fast, and an excellent swimmer.)

Writing Bragging and Boasting

Davy Crockett was the biggest boaster on the frontier. Have students write a short paragraph in which they use exaggeration to boast about their own abilities. They can begin by making a list of things they're good at. Start them off with suggestions such as running, swimming, playing a sport or a musical instrument, reading, spelling, and solving math problems.

Then have students think of ways they can exaggerate their skills. Can they compare their abilities to an animal, the way Davy did? Encourage them to use their imaginations to create the biggest boast ever.

Have students read aloud their boasts at a class Bragging and Boasting Contest. Students can score each boast on a scale from 1 to 10 based on how outrageous that boast is. Have students add up their own scores and divide by the number of judges to find each student's average score. The student with the highest score is the Biggest Bragger and Boaster of all!

Social Studies • Language Arts
Speak Out!

Davy Crockett was nervous about giving his first political speech, but it was an important one. Ask students to imagine that they are running for Congress. What would they say in a speech to convince people to vote for them?

1. Have students consider the following questions when preparing their speeches:

• What problems is our country facing? Which problems do you think need the most attention?

• What solutions can you think of for those problems?

• What could you do to make life better for the people in your state?

• A congressperson has to study issues, work with others to make decisions, and have the courage to fight for what he or she believes in. What qualities do you have that would make you a good congressperson?

2. Explain that after people hear their speech, they may only remember one or two things about it. Students may want to repeat certain points several times so they are easy to remember. Tell students that their speeches should be no longer than 2 minutes.

3. Have students write out their speeches. Give them an opportunity to practice speaking them aloud to other students, friends, or families (this is a great homework assignment). Students should time their speeches to make sure they are under 2 minutes.

4. Give each student an opportunity to read his or her speech in front of the class. You may wish to provide students with the option of tape recording their speech at home, and playing the tape for the class. Afterward ask: *Which speeches were most effective? Why?*

Resources

Davy Crockett and the Highwaymen: an historical novel by Ron Fontes and Justine Karman (Disney Press, 1992) Historical fiction brings Davy's incredible adventures to life.

The Narrow Escapes of Davy Crockett by Ariane Dewey (Greenwillow Press, 1990) An exciting nonfiction collection of Davy's most outrageous escapades.

Pecos Bill and Slue-Foot Sue

If you were to ask any cowhand to name the greatest cowboy to ever ride the Texas range, you'd be sure to hear the name Pecos Bill. Raised by coyotes until he was ten, young Bill quickly learned to ride horses and rope cattle better than anyone else in the state of Texas.

Pecos Bill loved his rope so much that he threw a lasso around anything in sight. He practiced on every bull, every cactus, and every critter in the state. He got so good at it that when a cyclone blew through the plains, Bill threw a lasso right around its middle, then jumped on its back and rode it across the dusty land.

One day, Bill was wandering under the hot Texas sun when he saw a bunch of cowhands watching a wild horse, a white mustang. Bill thought the horse was the most beautiful creature he had ever seen and wanted to tame it. The other cowhands warned him against it. They called the horse Widowmaker because every man who had tried to ride it had died trying.

That didn't stop Pecos Bill. After riding that cyclone there was nothing he couldn't do. Bill jumped on Widowmaker's back. The horse bucked and kicked, but Bill hung on tight. Before the sun sank, he had that horse tamed, and he made Widowmaker a promise that no one besides himself would ever be allowed to ride him.

Not long after, Bill was riding Widowmaker along the Rio Grande River when he saw the second most beautiful creature he had ever seen. A woman with hair as red as his own and eyes the color of a Texas bluebonnet was riding down the river on the back of a giant catfish. Bill couldn't believe his eyes.

The woman rode the catfish to shore and introduced herself as Slue-Foot Sue. It turned out that Sue could ride and rope as well as Bill himself, and could play the guitar around the campfire to boot.

Bill fell instantly in love, and asked Sue to marry him. She agreed, on one condition—that Bill let her ride Widowmaker. Bill didn't want to, but he agreed to let her ride him after their

wedding, hoping she'd forget.

But Sue didn't forget. Right after the wedding she headed for the horse. Sue didn't even wait to change out of her white wedding dress. A big bustle made of springs filled out the skirt in the back. As soon as Widowmaker felt Sue on his back he knew Bill had broken his promise. The horse bucked and kicked harder than he ever had before.

The force sent poor Sue flying up high in the sky, so high that people say they saw her go over the moon and come back down. Luckily, her thick bustle cushioned her fall, but it was so springy that she bounced right back up in the sky.

Bill was so heartbroken to see Sue go flying off again that he howled into the night so loud that he woke up everyone in Texas. Bill's coyote friends started howling too, and they still do to this day.

Now Bill knew that howling wouldn't bring Sue down, so he got out his rope, threw a lasso on her, and brought her back before she could bounce down again. Sue was shaken up, but she was all right.

On that trip over the moon Sue had learned a lot about the stars in the sky, and that came in handy soon after her wedding day. You see, Texas was in the middle of a terrible drought. It was so hot and dry that

folks perspired dust instead of sweat, and chickens laid eggs already fried. Bill knew things couldn't go on like that, but he didn't know what to do.

Sue had an idea. From her trip into space, she knew that the Big and Little Dippers were filled to the brim with clear, cool water. So she and Bill got the longest piece of rope they could find and climbed the highest mountain they could find. Then Bill threw a lasso around the handle of the Little Dipper. Sue grabbed ahold of the rope and together they pulled with all their might. The Dipper tipped just enough to send that clear, cool water pouring on Texas, and the drought ended.

To celebrate, Slue-Foot Sue played her guitar and Pecos Bill danced a jig, and for the rest of their days they roped and rode their way through the great state of Texas.

The End

Teaching Activities

About This Tale

While some researchers credit the stories of Pecos Bill and Slue-Foot Sue to the people of Texas, it is commonly believed that they were the creation of a writer named Edward O'Reilly, who wrote about their adventures in *Century* magazine beginning in 1923. O'Reilly was inspired by tall tale heroes like Davy Crockett and Paul Bunyan and, in Pecos Bill, set out to create a character bigger and more incredible than those two.

History Notes

In the 1860s, the cattle industry developed in Texas. Cattle were raised in the southern part of the state, and then every spring and fall the herds were led on long cattle drives to rail lines in Kansas, Nebraska, and Wyoming. The cowboy's job involved working on the ranch and driving the cattle safely to their destination. By the 1890s, when rail lines extended into Texas, the need for long cattle drives was gone and the heyday of the cowboy was over.

While Pecos Bill typifies the traditional cowboy to many, it's important to remember that about a third of cowboys were African American or Mexican American.

Vocabulary

bluebonnet: the bright-blue state flower of Texas

bustle: a wire framework that expands and supports the back of a woman's skirt. This fashion was popular in the 1800s.

cyclone: a funnel-shaped wind storm, also called a tornado

lasso: a rope with a loop at one end that tightens when the rope is pulled

Questions

1. What kinds of abilities might Pecos Bill have had after being raised by coyotes? (Answers may include: he could communicate with animals; he could fend for himself in the wild.) What two things was Bill best at? (roping and riding)

2. Can chickens really lay fried eggs? Why did the author use this image in the story? (It's an exaggerated image to show how very, very hot it was.)

3. In what way is Slue-Foot Sue like Sal Fink? (See page 24.) Answers may include: Sal Fink rode an alligator down a river; Sue rode a catfish.

Writing Tell a Witty Whopper

The image of Slue-Foot Sue bouncing up and down on her giant bustle is a funny one. In the Bill and Sue tales, as in most tall tales, humor plays a very important role. Lead students in a discussion to identify the humor in the story. (Sue bouncing on her bustle, chickens laying fried eggs, the Little Dipper being filled with water) Then challenge them to write a tale using humor and exaggeration—a real whopper. To help them along, write each of the following words or phrases on a small piece of paper and put the papers into a paper bag. (Feel free to add words of your own choice.) Have each student pick three words out of the bag, write them down, and return them to the bag. Those three words should appear in their story. Then let the fun begin!

elephant ● whipped cream ● roller skates ● bicycle ● flying saucer ● giant mouse ● teddy bear ● giant ● yodel ● yo-yo ● snake ● purple ● cyclone ● comet ● tickle ● sneeze ● snore ● star ● rainbow ● skunk ● stripes ●

pick-up truck ● cowgirl ● wrestler ● birthday cake ● balloon ● tail ● swimming pool ● tuba ● hiccup ● chocolate sauce ● jelly

Science Find the Little Dipper

The Big and Little Dippers were two of the earliest star groupings to be identified, partly because they are so easy to spot in the night sky. Invite students to go on a star search for them!

1. Copy, cut out, and distribute the Star Finder card below to each student.

2. Tell students to go outside on a clear, dark night with an adult family member and to bring along a flashlight, a pen or pencil, a book to lean on, and their Star Finder card. Suggest that they try to find a place away from tall buildings and bright lights,

if possible. Note: Because of Earth's rotation, constellations appear to change position during the year. The Star Finder card shows the Big Dipper in its position during the fall.

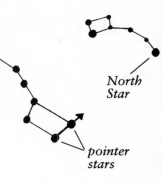

North Star

pointer stars

Resources

Cowboy by David H. Murdoch (Dorling Kindersley, 1993) This rich reference book is filled with photos and details about cowboy culture, from rope tricks to Stetson hats.

Texas by Dennis B. Fradin (Children's Press, 1992) Invite students to find out about the home state of Pecos Bill and Slue-Foot Sue with this book that includes a chronology of Texas history.

Star Finder

★ Use the drawing here to find the Big Dipper.

★ Find the two pointer stars on the right side of the dipper's "bowl."

★ Imagine that there is a straight line extending up from these two stars. Follow this line until you see a very bright star—the North Star. The North Star is the last star on the handle of the Little Dipper.

★ Look near the North Star for two other stars. They make up the "handle" of the Little Dipper. Below them are the four stars that make up the Little Dipper's "bowl."

★ Fill in the stars of the Little Dipper on the drawing.

Paul Bunyan

When Paul Bunyan was born in a cabin deep in the woods of Maine, he weighed a whopping 156 pounds. His parents weren't sure what to do with such a big baby, but soon Paul's destiny was clear to them. One night, as baby Paul tossed and turned in his cradle, the earth shook so much that four square miles of trees toppled to the ground. That was when the Bunyans knew that their son would grow up to be a logger.

And sure enough, that's what Paul did. By the time he was a teenager, Paul was taller than any tree in the forest and could easily chop down a tree with one blow. When he yelled "Tim-ber-r-r!!" his voice was so loud that two or three smaller trees would fall down as well.

Paul didn't want to let his talents go to waste, and besides, he was feeling a little cramped in the east. So he swung his axe over his shoulder and headed west, where Paul knew there were wide open spaces to live in and plenty of trees to chop down.

Along the way, Paul met a giant blue ox as long and wide as Paul was tall. Paul had never seen a blue ox before, and supposed it had turned blue during the Blizzard of Blue Snow a few winters back. Paul knew every good logger needed a strong animal to pull wagons loaded with logs from the forest to the

sawmill. Paul named the ox Babe and the two headed north and west.

Paul began logging the woods in Wisconsin. More than one thousand men worked in Paul's camp, including seven men almost as big as him. They were a loyal crew, and they liked working for Paul, not only because he was the biggest logger they had ever seen, but because he was smart, too. There wasn't a problem Paul Bunyan couldn't solve.

For one thing, when Paul got to the north, he found that the roads were all crooked. It was awfully difficult to run wagons of logs down those crooked roads. So Paul hooked up Babe's harness to the roads and had the big ox pull those roads until they were stick-straight.

Whenever there was a forest fire (which happened from time to time), Paul would lead Babe to the nearest river and ask the ox to drink that river dry. Then he'd lead Babe back to the fire, tickle Babe's stomach, and all that river water would come squirting back out and put out the fire.

After Paul had logged all that he could in Wisconsin, he headed to Minnesota. But Minnesota was a little too cold for him, so he headed to North Dakota next, and then finally as far north and west as Washington, Oregon, and California.

All the while, Paul's crew grew larger and larger. The hungry loggers ate so much that the camp cook needed a griddle one-quarter mile across just to cook their flapjacks in the morning. To get the grill greased up, he hired 17 boys to skate on it with slabs of bacon strapped to their feet like ice skates. When the flapjacks were cooked, the boys would hop on bicycles and ride down the quarter-mile-long table to deliver the pancakes before they cooled off.

To make pea soup for dinner, Paul had to help out by dumping the peas into a big lake and stirring up the mess until it was nice and thick.

Paul loved life at the logging camp, but every so often he would take off on a journey. Folks in Texas say Paul spent time digging the deepest oil wells in their state. Folks in Arizona say that Paul Bunyan dug the Grand Canyon for them in one day, and then decorated its walls with the crayons in his pockets. That's why the walls are so rich with beautiful colors today. In fact, wherever Paul traveled, people say he left his mark behind him.

What finally happened to Paul Bunyan? Some people say that he and his family are still living in the forests of the northwest. Others say that this world got too small for Paul Bunyan, and he figured out a way to visit some other planets for awhile. Wherever he is, you can be sure that he is leaving his mark there, too.

The End

Teaching Activities

About This Tale

The first story of Paul Bunyan was written in a newspaper article by a former logger in 1910. But Bunyan's fame really soared in the early 1920s, when the Red River Lumber Company used Paul's stories to sell their products. The creator of the advertising campaign, W.B. Laughhead, is credited with giving names to previously unnamed characters in the tales, including Babe, the Blue Ox.

History Notes

The logging industry that gave birth to Paul Bunyan began in the nineteenth century as Europeans turned to the vast, untouched forests of North America to fulfill their needs for timber. Early loggers used draft animals—working animals such as oxen and horses—to pull the logs out of the forest area. Then logs were often floated down streams to a sawmill or wood-products factory. Today, bulldozers and tractors have replaced draft animals in the forest, and trains and trucks transport logs instead of rivers.

Loggers today struggle with the problem of over-harvesting forests. Many environmentalists fear that too many trees are being harvested, endangering wildlife and air quality. Loggers, meanwhile, are worried about losing their livelihoods. It's a question that needs a Paul Bunyan-sized solution.

Vocabulary

destiny: something that a person is sure to do in the future

flapjack: pancake

griddle: a flat pan used on top of a stove

harness: straps fitted around a work animal so the animal can be led from one place to another

logger: a person who chops down trees for lumber

sawmill: the place where logs are sawed into smaller pieces to be used for lumber

Questions

1. Besides Paul's height, what else makes him a tall tale character? (answers may include: his big blue ox; his giant griddle; the fact that he helped make Texas oil wells and the Grand Canyon)

2. How were animals used in logging camps? (They pulled wagons filled with logs from the forest to the sawmill.)

3. Why did the cook's helpers strap bacon to their feet? (so they could grease the huge griddle)

4. Where do you think Paul Bunyan might still be today? (answers may include: places big enough to hide him, including forests, deserts, or even the moon)

Writing Natural Wonders

Legend has it that Paul dug the Grand Canyon in one day. People have always made up stories to explain how natural wonders were formed. Have students write their own tall tale starring Paul Bunyan. Their tale should explain how Paul formed one of our country's natural wonders. Have them base the tale on a natural geographic formation in your state or region, or share this list with students to get them started:

- The Great Lakes
- Hawaii's volcanoes
- The Rocky Mountains
- Niagara Falls
- The Great Salt Lake
- The Mojave Desert
- Old Faithful
- Monmouth Cave or Carlsbad Caverns

Geography Map Your State

If you were to look at the forests that Paul Bunyan logged on a map, you might see symbols like these: ▲▲▲. Maps sometimes use symbols to show at a glance where natural resources are located, where native animals live, and where important buildings are located. Your students can use symbols to make a map of your state.

Materials (for each student)
- 12-by-18-inch piece of craft paper
- pencil
- markers or colored pencils
- map or atlas

1. Ask students to draw an outline of your state on the paper. Suggest that they copy or trace it from a map or atlas.

2. Tell students to indicate any major lakes ⬯ or rivers ⌇.

3. Have students mark the locations of important cities and your community. Use a ★ to mark the state capital.

4. Have students use symbols like these to mark off natural areas, such as mountains, forests, and areas where crops are grown:

   ⌃⌃ mountains
   ▲▲▲ forests
   ✺✺✺ crops

5. Challenge students to add pictures of animals, famous people, and buildings on the map where they would be most likely to find them, adding as much detail as they like.

6. When students are finished, tell them to make a map key that explains what each symbol stands for. For example:

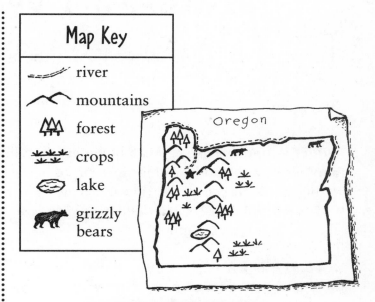

Map Key
- ⌇ river
- ⌃ mountains
- ▲▲▲ forest
- ✺✺✺ crops
- ⬯ lake
- 🐻 grizzly bears

Oregon

Reproducible Activity

Travel Paul Bunyan Country
(pages 46–47)

This activity helps students sharpen their map-reading skills.

Answers: 1. The Mississippi River; **2.** Minnesota; **3.** North Dakota and South Dakota; **4.** South Dakota; **5.** a border made by people; **6.** Montana; **7.** Washington; **8.** The Columbia River; **9.** About 300 miles; **10.** The Rocky Mountains

Resources

The Bunyans by Audrey Wood (Scholastic, 1996) In this picture book, the author invents original stories about Paul, his wife Carrie, and their children Little Jean and Teeny.

Paul Bunyan by Steven Kellogg (Mulberry, 1994) Another tall tale in the picture book series from author and illustrator Steven Kellogg.

Travel Paul Bunyan Country

The map on page 47 shows the northern states logged by Paul Bunyan and his crew. You can travel with Paul Bunyan across these states, but first check out these map-reading tips to help you on your journey:

Border A border (also called a boundary) is a line on a map that separates one area from another. Rivers and lakes may also make borders. Sometimes you'll see them on a map separating states and countries (like a squiggly line representing a river, instead of a straight line). Other natural borders or boundaries include mountains and forests, which are sometimes shown on maps as symbols.

Scale of Miles A scale of miles shows how distances on a map compare with actual distances on Earth. To use a map scale, hold the edge of a piece of paper between two points on a map and mark off how long the distance is. Then hold the paper up to the scale to find out how many miles the distance equals.

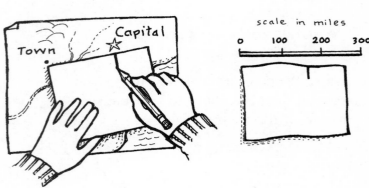

Time to Travel Fill in the answers to the questions below. Trace your route on the map as you go.

1. Start on the southern border of Wisconsin. What natural border will you need to cross to get to Iowa? _____

2. From Iowa's southern border, travel 300 miles north. What state are you in?

   _____

3. What two states border Minnesota to the west?_____

4. From Minnesota, cross the Red River to visit the state south of North Dakota. Write its name here._____

5. Travel from South Dakota to Wyoming. Will you cross a natural border, or one made by people?_____

6. Travel to the state that borders Wyoming to the north. Write its name here.

   _____

7. From the Rocky Mountains in Montana, travel 350 miles west. What state are you in? Write its name here._____

8. What river borders Washington to the south?_____

9. Travel from the Columbia River to the southern border of Oregon. About how many miles have you gone?_____

10. Travel east again. What natural border separates Idaho and Montana?_____

Teaching Tall Tales Scholastic Professional Books

Name _____

Paul Bunyan Country

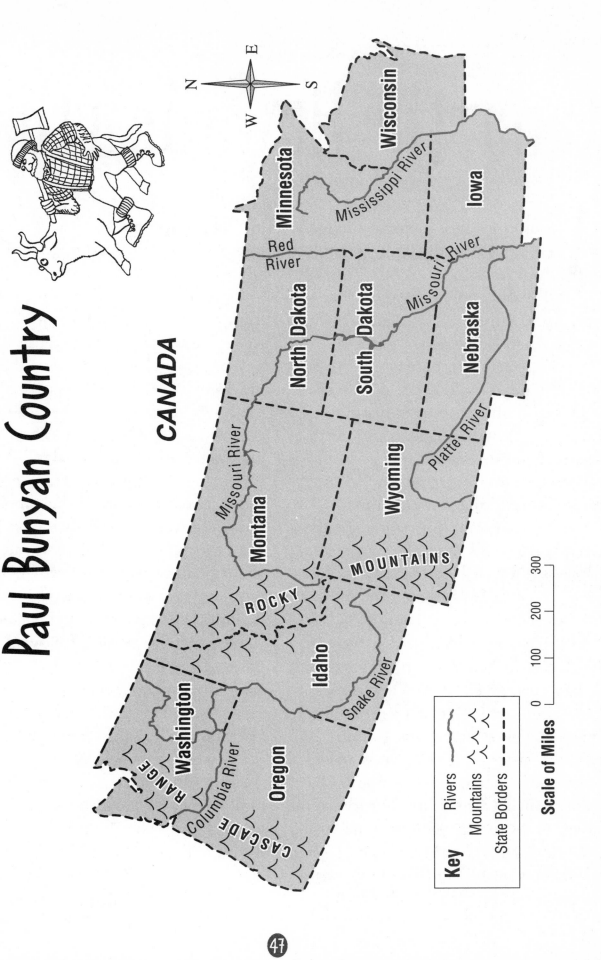

CANADA

N E S W (compass rose)

Minnesota

Wisconsin

Mississippi River

Iowa

Red River

North Dakota

Missouri River

South Dakota

Nebraska

Montana

Wyoming

Platte River

ROCKY

MOUNTAINS

Idaho

Snake River

Washington

Columbia River

Oregon

CASCADE RANGE

Key	
Rivers	～
Mountains	⋏ ⋏ ⋏
State Borders	– – –

Scale of Miles

0   100   200   300

Teaching Tall Tales Scholastic Professional Books

Kana, the Hawaiian Giant

A long time ago, a woman named Hina (HEE-nah) the Beautiful lived on the island of Hilo (HEE-loh) in Hawai'i (Hah-VY-ee). When she grew up, she married, and gave birth to a son named Kana (KAH-nah).

After Kana's birth he was sent to be raised by his grandmother on the island of Hawai'i. She knew right away that there was something special about the boy, and suspected that one of the gods had given him a great power. So she made a special mat for him out of vines, and covered him with a shelter of green leaves, and she fed him for 40 days. And for each of those days, Kana grew a foot taller, so when the 40 days were over he stood 40 feet tall.

As Kana grew older, he discovered that his great height wasn't the only gift he had been given. If he wanted to, Kana could make himself as small as the tiniest ant, or stretch himself until his head was as high as the clouds and his body was as narrow as a snake's. His grandmother warned him not to use this power unless it was an emergency.

While Kana was still a boy, Hina had one more son, Niheu (Nee-HAY-oo). He wasn't as tall as his older brother, but their grandmother knew that this boy was filled with courage and strength.

Soon after Niheu was born, a terrible thing happened. Chief Kaupipi Kapepe'ekauila (KOW-pee-pee KAH-pay-pay-ay-kah-oo-ee-lah) of the island of Moloka'i (Moh-loh-KY-ee) kidnapped the boy's mother, Hina, because he admired her great beauty. The Chief kept her trapped on his island on the mysterious Ha'upu (HAH-oo-poo) Hill.

The two boys missed their mother, but there was nothing they could do until they grew up. Niheu spent the years plotting ways to rescue his mother. Kana spent his days eating and sleeping. His favorite meal was 40 bowls of delicious poi, followed by a nice long nap.

Finally the day came that Niheu and Kana were men. Niheu tickled his brother's foot with a palm leaf until Kana woke up.

Kana rubbed the sleep from his eyes and listened to Niheu's plan. To get to the island of Moloka'i they would need a canoe. Kana hollowed out the tallest tree he could find and set it in the water. Then he pulled the second tallest

tree he could find from the ground to use as a club.

Kana and Niheu climbed into the giant canoe and began paddling to Moloka'i. Before long, Kana fell asleep. Chief Kaupipi knew the sons were coming to rescue their mother, and he sent many obstacles to try to stop them—a giant wave to drown them, a rocky ledge to crush them, and a monstrous fish to eat them. Each time disaster neared, Niheu woke up his brother, and Kana used his club to split the wave, turn the rocky ledge to dust, and send the fish flying across the ocean.

When they finally reached Moloka'i, they saw Ha'upu Hill rising from the shores, surrounded by misty white clouds. Niheu woke his brother and Kana climbed out of the canoe and stomped over to the island. As he approached it, the island began to float high in the air.

Kana knew this was an emergency, so he used his powers to stretch himself higher and higher, until his head was above the clouds and

his body was as thin as a snake's. When he finally reached the top of the mountain, he was so weak from hunger that he could not fight Chief Kaupipi. There was nothing he could do.

Niheu rowed Kana back to Hawai'i, where their grandmother fed Kana 40 bowls of poi. Then she told him the secret of Ha'upu Hill— it was held up by two giant turtles. To prevent the hill from rising into the sky, Kana would have to step on the turtles' backs.

So Niheu and Kana rowed back to Moloka'i and they approached Ha'upu Hill once more. This time, when the hill began to rise into the sky, Kana stepped on the backs of the turtles and the hill fell to the ground with a thud. Kana grabbed the hut on the top of the hill where his mother was trapped. He set his mother down safely in the canoe and told Niheu to row her back to Hawai'i.

When his mother and Niheu had left, Kana smashed the hill with his giant fist. The hill broke apart into 100 small turtles, who fell into the ocean and swam away.

The End

Teaching Activities

About This Tale

The Hawaiian Islands boast a rich tradition of folklore. The tale of Kana has many elements of a myth, but the exaggeration in the story and Kana's great height and abilities make him a cousin to many tall tale characters. His story and many other Hawaiian tales and legends were first written down in 1888 in *The Legends and Myths of Hawaii* by His Hawaiian Majesty King David Kalakua (Kah-LAH-kah-oo-ah).

History Notes

The Hawaiian islands lie in the Pacific Ocean about 2,400 miles southwest of California. The traditional name Hawaiians have for their island nation is "Hawai'i," from which the English name has been adapted. It is believed that the first colonists came from other islands in about the year 750. In 1810, King Kamehameha I (Kah-MAY-hah-MAY-hah) gained control over the islands' chiefs, uniting the islands under one government. That system lasted until 1893, when American residents, who had a stake in the island's sugar industry, deposed the reigning queen, Lili'uokalani (LIL-ee-oo-oh-kah-lah-nee). In 1898, Hawaii was annexed by the United States, and became our country's 50th state on August 21, 1959.

Vocabulary

canoe: a long, narrow boat that comes to a point at both ends

obstacle: something blocking the way

poi: a traditional Hawaiian dish made of the mashed root of the taro plant

Questions

1. What super abilities did Kana have? (He was 40 feet tall; he could shrink or stretch his body in emergencies.)

2. How did Kana finally rescue his mother from the island? (He learned that the island was held up by two turtles, and he stepped on their backs to keep it from floating into the sky.)

3. Do you think Kana could have rescued his mother without Niheu's help? Why or why not? (Answers will vary, but students may argue that without Niheu's brains, Kana's powers would do no good.)

4. What other tall tale heroes does Kana remind you of? (Answers may include: He was a giant, like Paul Bunyan and Old Stormalong.)

5. If you had a problem to solve, would you ask Niheu or Kana to help you? Explain your choice. (Answers will vary, but some students may prefer Kana's height and powers over Niheu's brains and perserverance, and vice versa.)

Writing Stretching the Truth

Kana was told to use his special shrinking and stretching abilities in an emergency. But what if he could use his powers all the time? Ask students to imagine that they have Kana's special stretching and shrinking powers. How would they use them? Have them write a short story describing their adventures. To get them started, suggest several situations; for example, they could stretch to reach things off of high shelves, dunk basketballs, or look for birds' nests in the trees; they could shrink to get an ant's-eye view of the world, or spy on others without being seen.

Math Breakfast for a Giant

Forty-foot-tall Kana ate forty times more than what a normal man would eat. Have students imagine that Kana is coming over for breakfast. Give them the list of ingredients below showing a typical breakfast for one person. Challenge students to figure out how much of each item to buy to feed Kana, and write out a shopping list. Encourage them to convert some of the measurements to larger-sized containers for easy carrying. For example, instead of buying 40 pints of milk, it would be easier to buy 5 gallons.

Ingredients
- 1 mango
- 1 cup of milk
- 1 pint of pineapple juice
- 3 eggs
- 2 muffins
- 6 ounces of cereal

ingredients
40 mangoes
40 cups milk
20 quarts
  pineapple
  juice
10 dozen eggs
80 muffins
15 pounds cereal

This list translates to: 40 mangoes; 40 cups, 10 quarts, or 2 1/2 gallons of milk; 20 quarts, 40 pints, or 5 gallons of pineapple juice; 10 dozen or 120 eggs; 80 muffins; and 15 pounds or 240 ounces of cereal.

Geography Make a Travel Guide

Ask students to imagine that they are planning to visit Hawaii, or that a friend is coming to visit them there. What places would they visit? How would they get around? What kinds of clothes should they bring? A travel guide can answer these questions and more. Have students follow these directions to make a brochure about the 50th state.

Materials
- Paper and pencils
- Paint, markers, colored pencils

1. Tell students to research the state in encyclopedias, atlases, travel books, magazines, or on the Internet. If possible, visit a travel agent to get more information.

2. Each travel brochure should answer the following questions. (Students can also add other facts that they think are interesting.)

   - What is the climate like?
   - What is the best way to get there? What about getting from one place to another?
   - What are some important cities?
   - Which animals and plants can be found in the state?
   - What are some traditional foods?
   - What are some natural wonders to visit?
   - What are the people of Hawaii like?

3. After students have all their information, ask them to organize it. Sections of their guides might have titles like Food, Getting Around, or Places to Visit.

4. Have students write up the information for each section of their guide, and illustrate the pages with drawings, cut-out pictures, and photos, including a cover.

Resources

Hawaii by Dennis B. Fradin (Children's Press, 1994) Part of the popular *From Sea to Shining Sea* series, this nonfiction book is packed with facts about the state.

Hawaiian Tales of Heroes and Champions by Vivian L. Thompson (Holiday House, 1971) This collection by Thompson, a Hawaiian resident and folklorist, is worth searching for in your library.

Sedna of the Sea

Many ages ago, Sedna lived on the shores of Alaska with her father and brothers. When she was old enough to be married, many men came to court her. They brought her gifts of warm furs and tasty fish from the sea. But Sedna did not want to marry any of them. She didn't want to be married to anyone. When her suitors tried to speak to her, Sedna turned her back and wouldn't reply.

Now, in those days, Sedna's behavior was unheard of. No woman had ever rejected so many marriage proposals. And this made her father very, very angry. He told Sedna that if she did not choose a husband soon, he would choose one for her.

Sedna knew her father meant what he said, and she didn't know what to do. She was sure she would never meet a man worth marrying.

But the very next day, a strange man sailed to shore in a large kayak. He was covered from head to foot in dark, warm furs. Wooden snow goggles covered his eyes. Sedna couldn't even see his face.

The suitor was certainly mysterious, and Sedna thought that he just might be different from all the rest. He sang Sedna a beautiful song about his home far away on a great island, and promised Sedna that she would eat the finest food and wear the finest furs if she married him.

The suitor's song won Sedna over, and she agreed to marry him. After all, she thought, her father would only choose someone much worse. As soon as the ceremony was over, they hopped into his kayak and sailed away.

The kayak traveled for miles and miles, until finally it rested on the shores of a large rocky cliff. Sedna couldn't see any trees or plants anywhere. This made her nervous. Was this the great island her husband had sung about?

Sedna's husband climbed out of the kayak and led her up the cliff to a large nest of twigs and branches. Sedna couldn't believe her eyes. Was this the beautiful home her husband had sung about?

Finally, Sedna's husband took off his fur robes and his wooden goggles, and Sedna saw in horror that there was no man under those robes, but a petrel with beady eyes and sharp claws. She

had been tricked into marrying a bird!

Sedna was miserable. She spent each day after that staring out into the lonely sea. One day, when the petrel was out catching fish, she spotted her father and brothers hunting on the waves. Sedna ran to the shore as fast as she could and called out to them.

When her father heard what had happened, he felt sorry for forcing Sedna into marriage and agreed to take her away from her rocky prison. They paddled away as fast as they could, just as the storm-black bird appeared overhead, screaming angrily.

The angry bird swooped out of the sky and pecked at Sedna's father with its sharp beak, and scratched at him with its claws. Sedna's father panicked. He knew the bird wanted Sedna back, so he threw his daughter into the sea.

The icy water froze Sedna down to her very bones. She tried to climb back into the kayak, but her terrified father struck at her hands with his paddle. The tips of her fingers snapped off like icicles. When they fell into the water they turned into the first seals and swam away.

Sedna tried to climb back into the kayak again, but her brothers, frightened of what they had seen, pried her fingers off. The bottoms of her fingers snapped off and turned into the first walruses when they hit the water.

One last time, Sedna tried to climb into the kayak with her thumbs. But they were not strong enough to support her, and they snapped off and became the world's first whales.

So Sedna fell into the deep sea, where she became the mother of all sea creatures. She still lives under the icy waters, and when she remembers the way her father and brothers treated her, she becomes angry and causes waves and storms.

The End

Teaching Activities

About This Tale

This Inuit tale is a myth that explains how some of the creatures of the sea came to be. Unlike a tall tale, it doesn't feature the elements of humor and exaggeration. Sedna's story is included in this book because the native peoples of North America have a rich tradition of folktale and myth, and Sedna's tale in many ways typifies those stories. Use the tale to have students compare myths and tall tales.

History Notes

Twice the size of Texas, Alaska is the largest state in the United States. It's also the northernmost state. Alaska was purchased from the Russians in 1867, and became our 49th state on January 3, 1959. The history of the Eskimo, or Inuit, people goes back at least 10,000 years to the end of the last ice age, when the first evidence of human settlement of Alaska appear. The Inupiaq Inuits, who live in the Arctic region, and the Sugpiaq Inuits in western Alaska survived by hunting sea mammals, especially whales, walruses, and seals. The Sedna myth rose out of this important aspect of Inuit culture.

Vocabulary

court: to seek someone's affections

kayak: a canoe made of a frame covered with animal skins

petrel: a sea bird that has the ability to fly far from land

suitor: a person who wants to marry someone

Questions

1. Why did Sedna agree to marry the mysterious stranger? (If she didn't choose a suitor, her father was going to choose for her; she was won over by his beautiful song.)

2. How did the petrel trick Sedna? (He disguised himself in furs and goggles; he lied to her in his song.)

3. Was the petrel's home what Sedna expected it to be? How was it different? (Sedna was expecting warmth and luxury; the petrel lived in a nest of twigs on a rocky cliff.)

4. Why didn't Sedna's father let her back into the boat? (He was afraid of the petrel.)

5. Sedna's tale is a myth. Compare her story to the others that you've read. What are some differences between myths and tall tales? What other myths have you heard or read? (Answers may include: Myths explain the origin of natural phenomena—in this story, how sea creatures came to be; tall tales are funny and use exaggeration.)

Writing | Make a Myth

A creation myth is a story passed down by a people to explain how something in nature was first created, such as thunder, fire, or an animal. Sedna's tale explains how seals, walruses, and whales came to be. Have students choose an animal or a natural phenomenon and make up their own myth explaining how it was created. For inspiration, you may wish to have students read other North American creation myths, such as *The Legend of the Bluebonnet* by Tomie DePaola (Putnam, 1983).

Science • Social Studies • Art | Alaskan Animal Mobile

The Sedna myth talks about seals, walruses, and whales. These animals were important for the survival of the Inuit people. But these aren't the only animals that the people of Alaska have depended on for food, clothing, and shelter. Students can research animals native to Alaska and display their results on a mobile.

Materials
- white cardboard or poster board
- paints, markers, or colored pencils
- scissors
- string
- thin dowels or sticks

1. Challenge students to use encyclopedias, almanacs, and nonfiction books about Alaska to find out which animals are native to this state. Tell them to research both sea and land animals.

2. Have students make a list of all the animals they've found, then find out how each animal was (or still is) important to the native people of Alaska. Was the animal hunted? If so, what was it used for?

3. Have students choose at least six animals for a mobile. Tell them to draw a picture of each animal on a piece of white cardboard and cut it out. (Each picture should be at least 5 inches wide and 5 inches high.)

4. Instruct students to write the animal's name on the back of each animal, then list the ways in which native peoples used the animal. For example:

Walrus
- blubber for fuel
- meat for food
- skin for clothing and shelter
- tusks for tools

5. Have students punch a hole through the top of each animal and tie a piece of string through the hole, then attach each animal to a dowel or stick. Let students experiment tying the animals to different sticks and at different lengths so that some hang higher or lower than others.

6. Tell students to give their mobile a title, such as "Animals of Alaska" or "Creatures of the North." Have them write the title on a card and tape it to or hang it from the very top of the mobile.

7. Hang the mobiles from the ceiling and let the animal facts fly!

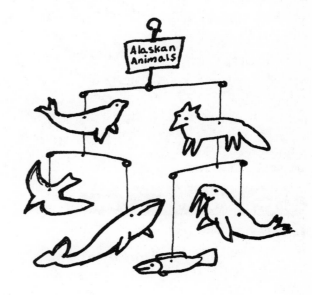

Resources

The Boy Who Found the Light: Eskimo Folktales by Dale DeArmond (Little, Brown, 1990) This illustrated collection of traditional Eskimo tales includes wood engravings by the author.

Eskimo Boy: Life of an Inupiaq Eskimo Village by Russ Kendall (Scholastic, 1992) Students can learn about contemporary Eskimo life from this photo essay.

Tall Tales Across the U.S.A. Poster

The Tall Tales Across the U.S.A. poster can be used as a focal and reference point for your tall tale lessons and, with the reproducible game cards on pages 58–62, can also be used as a fun, interactive geography game.

Using the Poster as a Game

Goal

To win the game, students use the map to answer geography or story-related questions on game cards. The winner is the first player to earn five game cards, by correctly answering questions about five different tall tale characters.

Materials

- Tall Tales Across the U.S.A. poster (bound into the back of the book)
- Game Rules (reproducible page 57)
- Question Cards (reproducible pages 58–62)
- small paper plate
- large paper clip
- pencil
- game pieces (use a different colored button for each player, or use game pieces from an old board game)
- scissors
- glue or paste

Preparation

1. Copy the Game Rules (page 57) and store with the game, or give a copy to each student. You may wish to read the rules ahead of time so you'll be familiar with the game.

2. To make the Question Cards, copy pages 58 to 62. Cut out each card along the dotted lines, then fold on the solid line to create a double-sided card. Paste the two sides together to form one card.

3. To make the spinner, copy the pattern here onto a small paper plate. To spin, students position the paper clip and pencil as shown, and flick the paper clip.

4. You may wish to review map reading skills such as reading a compass rose, identifying borders, and recognizing map symbols before students play the game.

Variations

1. Challenge students to create additional game cards with their own questions and answers.

2. Increase from five to ten the number of cards needed to win.

Game Rules

Players

2 to 4 players

Object of the Game

To collect a question card from 5 different tall tale characters.

How to Play

1. Each player chooses a different colored playing piece. Place all playing pieces on the state of Kansas.

2. Place the 40 Game Cards, question side up, on top of the characters they match on the map. (There will be four cards for each character.)

3. Take turns spinning the spinner. The first player to land on "N" goes first.

4. Spin the spinner again and move your playing piece in the direction shown to one of the card piles on the map. For example, if your spinner lands between "N" and "E," you can move north and east of Kansas to Sal Fink, Johnny Appleseed, Davy Crockett, John Henry, or Old Stormalong. You can choose any card pile you want, as long as you follow the directions on the map. The other players can challenge you if they  think you've gone in the wrong direction. If you move in the wrong direction, you miss your turn.

5. Move your playing piece to the card pile and pick up the top card. Use the map or your recollection of the stories to help you answer the question. Then turn the card over for the answer.

6. If you are right, keep the card. Then it's the next player's turn.

7. If you didn't answer the question correctly, return it to the bottom of the card pile. The turn passes to the next player.

8. On your next turn, spin the spinner again and follow the directions to move your playing piece to the next card pile. Sometimes the spinner will land on a direction that you can't travel in. For example, if you're in Hawaii and the spinner lands between S and E, there is nowhere you can go. Lose a turn and hope for a better spin next time.

9. The winner is the first player to earn 5 game cards, by correctly answering questions about 5 different tall tale characters.

Old Stormalong

Question
How did Stormalong defeat the giant octopus?

Answer
He tied its arms into knots.

Old Stormalong

Question
What state borders Maine to the southwest?

Answer
New Hampshire

Old Stormalong

Question
What New England state is not part of the Atlantic Coast: Maine, Vermont, or New Hampshire?

Answer
Vermont

Old Stormalong

Question
What is the closest state to Maine that ends in a cape?

Answer
Massachusetts

John Henry

Question
What river borders West Virginia to the northwest?

Answer
The Ohio River

John Henry

Question
How many states border West Virginia?

Answer
5 (PA, OH, KY, VA, MD)

John Henry

Question
Who won the contest between John Henry and the steam drill?

Answer
John Henry won the contest.

John Henry

Question
True or False? West Virginia is southwest of Ohio.

Answer
False. West Virginia is southeast of Ohio.

Johnny Appleseed

Question
What lake borders Ohio to the north?

Answer
Lake Erie

Johnny Appleseed

Question
What appeared in the sky when Johnny Appleseed was born?

Answer
A rainbow

Johnny Appleseed

Question
From Pennsylvania, Johnny sent apple seeds west on two canoes. What river did he use?

Answer
The Ohio River

Johnny Appleseed

Question
What natural border would make it difficult for Johnny to walk from Ohio to Iowa?

Answer
The Mississippi River

Davy Crockett

Question
Could Davy have traveled on foot from Nashville to Jefferson City? Explain your answer.

Answer
No. He would have needed a boat to cross the Tennessee and Mississippi Rivers.

Davy Crockett

Question
What acts as a natural border between Tennessee and North Carolina?

Answer
The Appalachian Mountains

Davy Crockett

Question
Why did Davy Crockett go to Washington, D.C.?

Answer
He went there to serve as a member of Congress.

Davy Crockett

Question
If you traveled south from Nashville, what capital city would you reach?

Answer
Montgomery, Alabama

Sal Fink

Question

Are there more states east of the Mississippi River or west of the river?

Answer

East (26 states east of the river and 24 states west)

Sal Fink

Question

What two rivers would you take to travel from the capital of Missouri to the capital of Colorado?

Answer

The Missouri and Platte Rivers

Sal Fink

Question

How many states does the Mississippi River flow through?

Answer

10 (LA, MS, AK, TN, KY, MO, IL, IA, WI, MN)

Sal Fink

Question

True or False? Des Moines, Iowa is northwest of Jefferson City, Missouri.

Answer

True

Annie Christmas

Question

Into what body of water does the Mississippi River empty?

Answer

The Gulf of Mexico

Annie Christmas

Question

What is the nearest capital city north of Baton Rouge, Louisiana?

Answer

Jackson, Mississippi

Annie Christmas

Question

What state borders Louisiana to the west?

Answer

Texas

Annie Christmas

Question

After leaving the paddleboat, how did Annie get the keelboat safely back to New Orleans?

Answer

She tied the boat's rope around her waist and pulled it there herself.

Pecos Bill & Slue-Foot Sue

Question
True or False? The Rio Grande River acts as a border between Texas and New Mexico.

Answer
False

Pecos Bill & Slue-Foot Sue

Question
If you traveled north from Austin, what capital city would you reach?

Answer
Oklahoma City, Oklahoma

Pecos Bill & Slue-Foot Sue

Question
What body of water borders Texas to the east?

Answer
The Gulf of Mexico

Pecos Bill & Slue-Foot Sue

Question
What was Slue-Foot Sue riding when Pecos Bill first saw her?

Answer
A giant catfish

Paul Bunyan

Question
Paul left Oregon to drill for oil wells in Texas. In what direction did he travel?

Answer
Southeast

Paul Bunyan

Question
What was the name of Paul Bunyan's blue ox?

Answer
Babe

Paul Bunyan

Question
True or False? The capital of Idaho is farther east than the capital of Oregon.

Answer
True

Paul Bunyan

Question
What acts as a natural border between Washington and Oregon?

Answer
The Columbia River

Kana

Question
What is the largest Hawaiian island?

Answer
Hawaii

Kana

Question
Which is a shorter canoe trip: from Maui to Molokai, or Oahu to Kauai?

Answer
Maui to Molokai

Kana

Question
On which Hawaiian island can you find the state capital?

Answer
Oahu

Kana

Question
What was Kana's favorite meal?

Answer
40 bowls of poi

Sedna

Question
What three bodies of water border Alaska?

Answer
The Arctic Ocean, Bering Sea, and Gulf of Alaska

Sedna

Question
What kind of animal was Sedna's husband?

Answer
A kind of bird called a petrel

Sedna

Question
In what direction would you travel to get from the capital of Alaska to the Arctic Ocean?

Answer
North

Sedna

Question
According to the myth, what three sea animals grew from Sedna's fingers?

Answer
Seals, walruses, and whales

Wrapping up the Theme

Use these fun and engaging activities to wrap up your tall tales theme.

Language Arts • Math

Make a Tall Tale Character Chart

There are many common themes in the tall tales in this unit. Create a chart like the one below. Have students write "yes" in the box below the character's name if that element appears in the story. They'll write "no" if the element does not appear. You can fill in the chart as a class, or have each student complete it as an individual assignment.

Language Arts

Invent a Tall Tale Character

Tall tales were often written about popular or exciting occupations of the time. In this book alone, students encounter a sailor, a logger, a riverboat operator, and a railroad worker. Have students invent a tall tale character based on one of the occupations or hobbies listed below (or another of their choice). Some didn't exist when tall tales were popular; others haven't been turned into tall tales—until now.

- astronaut
- submarine captain
- computer programmer
- movie director
- teacher

- skateboarder
- archaeologist
- surfer
- mail carrier
- artist

Encourage students to include the details of the character's birth and childhood, a physical description of the character, and at least one tale of an amazing accomplishment.

Story Element	Old Stormalong	Johnny Appleseed	John Henry	Sal Fink	Annie Christmas	Davy Crockett	Pecos Bill	Slue-Foot Sue	Paul Bunyan	Kana	Sedna
was a giant											
an amazing thing happened at birth											
was kind to animals											
battled animals											
battled forces of nature											
had adventures on water											
traveled great distances											
saved someone who needed help											
was based on a real person											

Dig up a Tall Tale

The characters in this book aren't the only tall tale characters in our country's history. Have students research other tall tale characters. Ask them to choose one new character and write that character's tale in their own words. Possible characters include Mose, the New York fireman; Febold Febolsdon, the midwest farmer and inventor; and Sally Ann Thunder Whirlwind Crockett, Davy Crockett's adventurous wife. Students can illustrate their tales and add them to their tall tale storybooks.

Language Arts Tell a Story

In many cases, tall tales were passed down by storytellers from generation to generation. It takes practice to tell a story that will captivate an audience. Students can follow these steps to learn how to tell a story to the class:

1. Choose a tall tale story that interests you. It can be a story from your tall tale storybook, or another tall tale you know.

2. Storytellers usually tell stories in their own words. Rewrite the tale in *your* own words. Make it no longer than one or two pages.

3. Read the story aloud, slowly. What could you do to make the story more exciting? Some storytellers make gestures, talk in different voices, and use sound effects. For example, if you were telling the story of Old Stormalong, you might want to make gestures when Stormy talks about tying knots in the octopus's arms. Or you could make a windy noise in a story about Pecos Bill riding a cyclone. Underline the parts of the story where you might be able to add things like gestures and sound effects.

4. Practice telling your story until you have memorized it. Make sure you speak slowly and clearly, so that your audience will be able to understand you. Before telling your story to an audience, try it out on a friend or family member, or tape record it and play it back for yourself.

5. When it's time to tell your story, take a deep breath. Then get ready to have some storytelling fun!

Throw a Tall Tale Party

Plan a party to celebrate the completion of your tall tale theme. A party might be a good occasion to perform several of the activities in this book, such as making apple snacks (page 17), holding a bragging contest (page 37), and having a storytelling festival (page 64). You might also perform short plays based on one or more of the stories. Or read the tall tales aloud once again and lead children in a discussion: Who were their favorite characters? Which characters did they admire most?

Before the party, have students make costumes so they can come dressed as their favorite tall tale character. Students can also wear their tall tale character masks (page 30). Here are some simple suggestions:

Annie Christmas: Make a long necklace out of plastic beads.

John Henry: Make a sledgehammer out of long paper towel rolls and cardboard.

Sedna: Pin or tape paper seals, whales, and walruses to clothing.

Pecos Bill and Slue-Foot Sue: Make 10-gallon hats out of large pieces of construction paper.

Johnny Appleseed: Make a flour-sack shirt out of an old pillowcase.